Portraits

of

UNIQUE HOMES

VOLUME ONE
1992

Portraits
— of —
UNIQUE HOMES

Written by Shelley Nohowel

Edited by Richard A. Goodwin
With assistance from Kathleen Carlin,
Lauren Hauptman, Kenneth Hunt,
Susan L. Pisut and Ilene Schechter

Designed by Donald J. Tesoriero
and Alan Dittrich

Production by Carole A. Harley
and Angus Stopford

A UNIQUE HOMES PUBLICATION

Contents

Introduction
6

THE HOMES

Introduction

Even in fluctuating real estate markets, one thing remains constant: People are fascinated by other people's homes. This is especially true when the "other people" live in houses that fall within that vague and intriguing category known as luxury real estate. (I use the word "vague" because if I've learned anything after 10 years of writing about high-end properties and upscale real estate markets, it's that "luxury home" means different things to different people, and there exists no quintessential example to illustrate the term.)

For some, a home is only luxurious when it's filled with the latest appliances and a host of high-tech gadgets. For others, a beautifully restored antique residence rich in original details and character affords the ultimate living environment. And then, of course, there are those people who insist that the only way to go is a new house built to resemble an old house, boasting an interior with authentic antique details as well as the latest in high-tech gadgets. In this, our premier edition of *Portraits of Unique Homes*, we strive to celebrate that diversity by taking you on a tour of the finest properties that have appeared in the pages of *Unique Homes* magazine over the past year or so.

Those of us who worked on this book would like to thank the owners, architects and interior designers who shared their stories and insights, which not only made the text more interesting, but also illuminated the fact that the character of a home is determined by much more than wood, plaster and stone. Also, a special thank you to the real estate agents who helped provide us with the information needed to get the book written, and the photographers, whose work truly brings each property to life on the page.

We hope that by taking a journey with us into the world of these unique homes, you will be entertained, amused and even inspired.

Richard A. Goodwin

Richard A. Goodwin
Editor

Chase Manhattan Personal Financial Services

CALIFORNIA

Beverly Hills:	9150 Wilshire Boulevard	(310) 550-3333
Burlingame:	1440 Chapin Avenue	(415) 347-9595
Encino:	16830 Ventura Boulevard	(818) 382-6400
Indian Wells:	74-900 Highway 111	(619) 341-7017
La Jolla:	4365 Executive Drive	(619) 597-2700
Los Angeles:	801 South Grand Avenue	(213) 689-4542
Los Gatos:	16450 Los Gatos Boulevard	(408) 358-7370
Newport Beach:	3991 MacArthur Boulevard	(714) 760-2671
Orange:	3111 North Tustin Avenue	(714) 921-2441
Palo Alto:	200 Page Mill Road	(415) 329-8300
Pasadena:	2 North Lake Avenue	(818) 449-7744
San Diego:	501 West Broadway	(619) 525-1540
San Francisco:	101 California Street	(415) 398-5005
Santa Barbara:	1525 State Street	(805) 962-2775
Torrance:	3501 Sepulveda Boulevard	(310) 542-6767
Walnut Creek:	1600 South Main Plaza	(510) 947-1311

COLORADO

Aspen:	201 North Mill Street	(303) 920-3360
Denver:	2000 S. Colorado Boulevard	(303) 759-1411

CONNECTICUT

Avon:	111 Simsbury Road	(203) 677-7003
Norwalk:	501 Merritt Seven	(203) 846-1106

DELAWARE

In Delaware:	(800) 634-0581
Outside Delaware:	(215) 668-1224

FLORIDA

Boca Raton:	5355 Town Center Road	(407) 368-4644
Coral Gables:	Five Alhambra Plaza	(305) 443-2217
Fort Lauderdale:	200 E. Las Olas Boulevard	(305) 356-5125
Maitland:	2300 Maitland Center Parkway	(407) 660-2124
Naples:	800 Laurel Oak Drive	(813) 566-2520
Palm Beach:	218 Royal Palm Way	(407) 832-6601

GEORGIA

Atlanta:	3353 Peachtree Road, NE	(404) 814-2080

ILLINOIS

Northbrook:	707 Skokie Boulevard	(708) 564-9090
Oak Brook:	1420 Kensington Road	(708) 954-4690

MARYLAND

Chase Bank of Maryland   Member FDIC

Rockville:	6116 Executive Boulevard	(301) 984-9292

MASSACHUSETTS

Boston:	50 Milk Street	(617) 695-1430
Burlington:	24 New England Executive Park	(617) 273-1041
Centerville:	1645 Route 28	(508) 790-3232
Dedham:	One Dedham Place	(617) 461-0650

MICHIGAN

Bloomfield Hills:	100 Bloomfield Hills Parkway	(313) 645-6466

MINNESOTA

Chase Manhattan Financial Center, Inc.

Bloomington:	8300 Norman Center Drive	(612) 831-0006

NEW JERSEY

Marlton:	Five Greentree Centre	(609) 985-0770
Princeton:	101 Carnegie Center	(609) 987-9339
Red Bank:	230 Half Mile Road	(908) 219-9292
Ridgewood:	1200 East Ridgewood Avenue	(201) 652-2410
Short Hills:	51 John F. Kennedy Parkway	(201) 379-0440

NEW YORK

The Chase Manhattan Bank, N.A.   Member FDIC

Garden City:	1051 Franklin Avenue	(516) 248-3900
New York:	380 Madison Avenue	(212) 557-4300
Southampton:	67 Hampton Road	(516) 287-4520
White Plains:	1214 Mamaroneck Avenue	(914) 683-8730

OHIO

Cleveland:	1132 Terminal Tower	(216) 736-7777

OREGON

Lake Oswego:	5285 S.W. Meadows Road	(503) 684-7829

PENNSYLVANIA

Bala Cynwyd:	251 St. Asaphs Road	(215) 668-1224
Pittsburgh:	5700 Corporate Drive	(412) 369-1500
Trevose:	6 Neshaminy Interplex	(215) 244-1048

TEXAS

Austin:	9020 Capital of Texas Highway	(512) 346-4320
Dallas:	12720 Hillcrest Road	(214) 934-0199
Fort Worth:	1320 S. University Drive	(817) 877-1450
Houston:	1100 Milam Street	(713) 751-5655
	1800 West Loop South	(713) 871-0926

UTAH

Chase Manhattan of Utah

Salt Lake City:	2180 South 1300 East	(801) 466-1792

VIRGINIA

Vienna:	8300 Boone Boulevard	(703) 761-1425

WASHINGTON

Bellevue:	13555 S.E. 36th Street	(206) 562-8929

After business hours and 24 hours a day during weekends, please call the Chase Information Center℠ 1-800-AT-CHASE.

Why Jumbo Mortgage clients choose Chase.

Jumbo Mortgages tailored to fit your needs.

CHASE understands that purchasing a home is a complex process. At Chase, we place high value on making the real estate financing process as easy as possible. Our ease of process is just one of the reasons why we're a recognized leader in customer satisfaction, according to a recent nationwide mortgage financing survey.*

Here are some other reasons:

✓ *Flexible Financing Programs–Tailored to Your Needs.* Chase offers you a broad choice of programs and repayment options to accommodate your unique needs.

✓ *Large Loan Amounts.* Maximize your buying power with sizeable loan amounts up to $2 million or more, if you qualify.

✓ *Knowledgeable and Dependable Service.* Chase Relationship Managers are assigned to you on an exclusive basis to help you tailor a program around your objectives.

✓ *Fast Loan Decisions.* Your Relationship Manager has the expertise and authority to give you a conditional loan decision quickly.

✓ *Low Closing Costs.* Since we offer low points options, you may reduce your initial expenses substantially.

Clients ranked us number one for our easy application process, fast loan decisions, client-oriented Relationship Managers and tailored financing programs.*

For more information on mortgages up to $2 million or more, call the Chase Manhattan office located nearest you.

C H A S E   M A N H A T T A N.
P R O F I T   F R O M   T H E   E X P E R I E N C E.SM

* Source: Walker Customer Satisfaction Measurements, one of the Walker Research companies.

4257

Your pool in the valley, lake in the mountains, marina at the shore, stream on the farm...

All just one phone call away.

"Home" means so many different things to different people. For some, it is a palatial estate high atop a mountain, for others a rustic beachhouse on the shore. A ranch in Montana, a condo in Hawaii.

No matter what your taste, your lifestyle, or your location, there is most likely a CENTURY 21® office close at hand. That's because our network consists of more than 5000 offices, staffed with tens of thousands of real estate professionals ready to serve your needs.

Best of all, you can access this vast network with just one local phone call — to the CENTURY 21 office nearest you or toll-free 1-800-221-7920.

So whether you're moving around the corner or around the world, whether your needs are simple or complex, whether your tastes are extravagant or modest, there is no real estate sales organization better equipped to help you find the home of your dreams than the CENTURY 21 system.

It's no wonder that — year in and year out — the Brokers and Sales Associates of the CENTURY 21 system help sell more homes than any other real estate sales organization on earth.

1-800-221-7920

The Homes

Hope Island

— Casco Bay, Maine —

"After dressing for dinner everyone would gather on the porch for cocktails. There was an old school grace about it that you just don't see anymore. At about 6:45 p.m. someone would ring the ship's bell to give everyone time to top off their drinks, and at seven o'clock or so, we would all file in for dinner." When J. Bradford Harlow reminisces about summers spent on Hope Island, the story is rich in New England nostalgia. Bell buoys clanking in the choppy Atlantic. A path of wild roses leading to the 1914 summer "cottage" with its 13 bedrooms and six fireplaces. Excursions on the 38-foot lobster boat and sunbathing on the rocks. Clawfoot tubs and classic shutters. From the gables overlooking distant lighthouses to the four cords of wood neatly stacked outside the back door, the place is about as genteel a step back in time as one is likely to ever find.

On this 88-acre island off the coast of Portland, Maine, life may have relaxed to the extent that jackets and ties are no longer required at dinner, but there remains a sense of permanence that goes back over three generations, when the grandfather of Harlow's wife purchased Hope Island and, with two other investors, established the Hope Island Club. Memories of the early days are well chronicled in a history prepared back in 1959. There was once a staff of 14—the usual cook, butler, parlor maid, chambermaid and a nurse for each child. There was a horse and wagon ready to escort guests from Juanita, the family yacht, up from the dock to the main house. And there were the deer, quite inquisitive and unafraid, which would actually swim to Hope Island

from neighboring islands and stay for a month or two.

From the dock, the white clapboard house is about an eighth of a mile stroll along a boardwalk with a canopy of tall pines above. Reaching the high bluff at the southeast end of the island, you can look out from the large front porch, lift your face to the salty breezes and wonder if summers could possibly be any better than this.

Photography by D. J. Callighan.

Hope Island was presented in Unique Homes by LandVest, Portland, ME.

CHARACTERISTICS

Property size: Approximately 88-acre island in Casco Bay.
Architectural style: Classic New England seaside cottage.
When built: 1914, and continuously improved over the years.
Number of rooms: 24.
Number of bedrooms: 13, plus staff quarters.
Number of baths: Seven full, one half-bath.
Outbuildings: 14-room tenant farmhouse (early 1900s), generator house with workshop, large barn (circa 1915).
Distinctive features: Six fireplaces, glass doors opening to porches, claw foot tubs, old wood floors and wonderful water views throughout.
Additional highlights: Hope Island's 9,000 feet of waterfront include a 125-foot pier and four beaches; miles of walking paths and roadways. A separate, smaller island just off the northern coast is included.

OPPOSITE TOP: *A large stone fireplace makes the living room a popular gathering spot on chilly Maine evenings.* OPPOSITE BOTTOM: *Hope Island as seen from the air.* ABOVE: *This classic "cottage" by architects Bissel, Sinkler & Tilden contains some 10,400 square feet of space.* RIGHT: *Main house accommodations consist of 13 bedrooms.* BELOW: *The perfect spot to enjoy the panoramic views over Casco Bay.*

Cachet in the Back Bay

Boston, Massachusetts

Tiffany and Walter James never park their car when they come home to their residence overlooking the Boston Public Garden. They never carry their groceries or packages inside, nor do they stand in line for theatre tickets. When it's time for a massage in the European spa or a complete health club workout, it's no further than their elevator. Dinner can be intimate and at home, or downstairs at Biba, an electric bistro with cuisine by Lydia Shire, 1992 winner of the coveted James Beard award given to the "Best Chef in the Northeast."

The Jameses oversee a multi-million-dollar lingerie empire with offices in the United States, Canada and the United Kingdom; and in Boston, they have found a home that sensibly eases the demands of a harried executive schedule with a staff that includes valet parkers and door attendants, a concierge and major domo, plus quick-to-the-call services such as gardening, housekeeping, dry cleaning and pantry stocking. The much-publicized building known as The Heritage on the Garden fronts the corner of

OPPOSITE: *Spacious enough to accommodate large-scale gatherings, the private, landscaped terrace overlooks a wonderful Boston panorama that includes the Public Garden.* LEFT: *The facade of The Heritage on the Garden, which the Boston Globe referred to as "a model of what an urban building ought to be."* BELOW: *Guests are greeted by a "rain forest" of copper, gold leaf and bronze, sculpted by one of the few artisans still practicing this art.*

CHARACTERISTICS

Architectural style: Contemporary condominium in The Heritage on the Garden.
When built: The Heritage on the Garden was completed in the late 1980s.
Square footage: 5,074 (interior space), 1,374 (terrace).
Distinctive features: Extensive use of marble, copper, gold leaf and bronze—all work customized for this apartment residence. The private, landscaped terrace affords beautiful views of the Public Garden.
Special amenities: Building services include state-of-the-art security, door attendants, valet parking, concierge, major domo, plus arrangements for housekeeping, laundering, dry cleaning, pantry-stocking and more.
Additional highlights: Heritage on the Garden is Boston's premier mixed-use building, with luxury offices on lower floors, and outstanding shops and restaurants on the street level. The European spa, Le Pli, is also in the building.

BELOW: *Patterned marble flooring and marble columns add to the cool sophistication of the interior spaces. Behind the drapery sheers, celebrated views of Boston await.* OPPOSITE TOP: *The residence was custom designed by its owners to offer a completely different feel than the typical luxury Boston brownstone. The result is a striking residence where a decidedly contemporary ambience is infused with a level of artistry seldom seen in newer construction.* OPPOSITE BOTTOM: *The state-of-the-art lighting system is used to great effect in the formal dining area.*

Arlington and Boylston Streets at the edge of the historic Back Bay, sharing its address with some 125,000 square feet of executive office space and elite retailers including Escada, Hermes, Sonia Rykiel and Waterford.

The *Boston Globe* called it "as handsome and inviting an addition to the public streetscape as any piece of architecture in recent years." The *New York Times* said: "Brick, limestone, granite and copper exterior detailing, glass and mahogany storefronts, and double acorn streetlights give The Heritage an aura of the elegant past associated with the Back Bay." The building is regarded as a triumph for the community, but few relish in its luxuries more than the people who live here, among them Tiffany and Walter James.

Theirs is a 5,000-square-foot urban aerie with an additional 1,400 square feet of outdoor terrace overlooking the Garden's treetops and famous swan boats. It's a front-row view on four seasons from five lustrous banks of windows. The copper and gold wall sculptures were designed by Mr. James in collaboration with a Hawaiian architect. Sleek marble surfaces are tempered by soft fabrics and deep carpets. The custom lighting is capable of many moods, and all bring an elegant drama to the interior. Outdoors, a profusion of trees and flowers frames a cherished Boston view.

There is a certain satisfaction in stepping off the private-access elevator, walking through a columned allée of rose marble, and discovering the toughest decision of the afternoon may be whether to get comfortable on a chaise in the sun, or join a few others in the Great Library for tea. As Tiffany and Walter James have learned, life here can be very kind indeed.

Photography by Arlene B. Curley.

This ultimate Boston address was presented in Unique Homes by Arlene B. Curley, Arlene B. Curley Real Estate, Boston, MA.

Ocean Lawn

Newport, Rhode Island

Much has been written of the halcyon days of Newport and the extravagances of a summer colony filled with Vanderbilts, Astors and Belmonts. Caviar was fed to the dogs, while horses were stabled in barns built by Stanford White. The thirst for spending the most money in the shortest period of time was unquenchable. In the 1600s, this seacoast town provided sanctuary for religious refugees from Boston. By the mid-18th century, it was a center for "individual opulence, learning and liberal leisure." Following the Revolution, there came a hundred years of healing, but by the late 19th century, Newport was once again the great watering hole of the Northeastern elite.

To house as much to as amuse the great lords of the mines, railroads and Wall Street, mansions were built on great parcels overlooking the sea. Mrs. Herman Oerlich's "Rosecliff" was adapted from Le Trianon at Versailles. Oliver Belmont's "Belcourt Castle" was a lavish Medieval fantasy inspired by a hunting lodge built by Louis XIII.

OPPOSITE: *Since it was built, circa 1889, the stately brick "cottage" known as Ocean Lawn has commanded a magnificent setting overlooking the ocean in the fabled watering hole of Newport. From the awning-covered terrace, a green carpet of lawn rolls down to the sea.*
LEFT & BELOW: *Brilliant with color in summer, the formal gardens at Ocean Lawn are like an enormous outdoor living room where masses of flowers and an array of magnificent trees seem to thrive on the mild sea air.*

🏛

Characteristics

Architectural style: Queen Anne brick "cottage."
When built: Circa 1889. Purchased by Mr. and Mrs. Harvey S. Firestone, Jr. in the early 1950s; expertly maintained ever since.
Number of rooms: Approximately 20.
Number of bedrooms: Eight, plus four for staff.
Number of baths: Eight and one-half.
Outbuildings: Brick carriage house, children's playhouse with kitchen and bath, greenhouse.
Distinctive features: Extensive oak paneling, Portuguese tiles, hand-carved mantels, handmade shutters, and skylighted stairhall off upstairs bedrooms. Marvelous workmanship throughout by the eminent architectural firm of Peabody and Stearns. Double libraries ("his" in oak, "hers" in 18th century English pine), drawing room with Louis XV marble mantel, dining room with Adam-style mantel, fireplaces in four of the bedrooms, and a wine cellar.
Additional highlights: Ocean Lawn has always been considered one of the great summer "cottages" of Newport. Large expanses of lawn, an awning-covered terrace overlooking the sea, a swimming pool and abundant flowers embellish this historic estate.

OPPOSITE TOP: *Antique Portuguese tile surrounds the fireplace in the oak-paneled sitting room, originally "his" library.* OPPOSITE BOTTOM: *"Her" library is warmly appointed with antique pine paneling brought from England.* LEFT & BELOW: *The drawing room is a magnificent entertaining space with its painted French paneling and Louis XV marble mantel.*

Henry Vanderbilt's "The Breakers," patterned in the style of the 17th century palaces of Genoa, came complete with its own verdant park designed by Frederick Law Olmsted. No less elaborate in scope was the Ives-Gammel summer compound on "The Cliffs," consisting of four private houses built in the last half of the 19th century: Southside, Cliff Side, Hopedene and Ocean Lawn, the last of which was purchased by Mr. and Mrs Harvey S. Firestone, Jr. in the early 1950s.

Each of these four residences took on an elaborate style of its own, be it the compound's original Italianate villa with its grand piazza and great promise for summertime fun, or the massive brick Queen Anne cottage built in 1889 by Peabody and Stearns of Boston for R. H. Ives' daughter, Mrs. Gammell, and given the name "Ocean Lawn." The firm had previously established a fine reputation in Newport with various other projects, including Pierre Lorrilard's "The Breakers" and F. W. Vanderbilt's "Rough Point."

It is known that Mrs. Gammel reviewed a host of other designs for Ocean Lawn, including those submitted by Richard Morris Hunt and McKim, Mead &

RIGHT: *Each of the two elegantly appointed bedrooms that comprise the master suite has a fireplace, private bath and generous closet space.* OPPOSITE TOP & BOTTOM: *Both "his" and "her" libraries were designed to provide display areas for Mrs. Firestone's world-renowned collection of French porcelain.*

White, before selecting Peabody and Stearn's proposal for the home, which would keep no less than 24 masons and 15 carpenters busy during the summer of 1888. The interiors were completed the following winter; and by the spring of 1889, painting, decorating and landscaping were well under way.

The past century has served only to mellow the estate with its great sweeping lawns leading to the sea, thanks in large measure to the efforts of its most recent owner, Bette Parke Firestone, who artfully maintained and embellished Ocean Lawn for approximately 40 years.

Interiors acquired the fine patina of antique paneling. Windows were fitted with handmade shutters. European imports were extensively incorporated within the home, including the entry gates and lights which were custom made in France.

Ocean Lawn provided a showplace befitting black tie dinners, fancy dress teas and indulgent summers of seaside leisure. But the home also served as a museum-like backdrop for Mrs. Firestone's superb art and antiques, as well as her world-renowned collection of French silver and porcelain. Sèvres plates rested in the carved niches

of "her" library panelled in 18th century English pine ("his" library was all warm oak). Public rooms were filled with the fragrance of flowers cut from the extensive gardens. Lustrous silks and brocades glowed in sunshine and firelight. All was old English and grand, but spirited with the style of a great American lady.

In a letter to Mrs. Firestone dated 1984, Mr. David Chase—a researcher who had documented the ancestry of Ocean Lawn—completed his five-page chronicle with: "Such is the early history of Ocean Lawn and its environs as I know it. Of course, I have said little about the life lived here—and that is just as well, for you know that story better than I." Such has been the way with the great houses of Newport; every sconce and staircase noted, every facade and garden photographed a thousand times over. But the lives of its owners remain, as is the way in Newport, pamperingly private.

Photography by John Hopf and William Leatherman.

Ocean Lawn was presented in Unique Homes by Robert Corbin, Private Properties, Newport, RI.

Canaan Manor

Greenwich, Connecticut

Owning a residence that is considered a work of art has both its rewards and its responsibilities, as Stephen Nichols learned so well when he purchased and occupied an Addison Mizner villa in Palm Beach several years ago. The uniqueness of concept, craft and artistry in such a home, along with the attention a historic house of some 15,000 square feet requires, largely inspired this man of many talents to create an architectural statement all his own. But the home he and his wife, Margaret, came to build in the "back country" of Greenwich, Connecticut, was far more than a grand exercise in construction. On every level, it evolved as a home of high-tech advantage and age-old European character.

The estate, which came to be known as "Canaan Manor," began with the perfect setting in Conyers Farm, a 1,400-acre enclave of woodlands, lake waters, polo fields and utmost privacy just over an hour from New York City. After much looking in this quiet sanctuary of the corporate and entrepreneurial elite, the Nicholses began their four-year project on a site of nearly 15 acres with its own private island on 125-acre Converse Lake.

OPPOSITE TOP & BOTTOM: *The handsome stone facade of Canaan Manor fits in beautifully with the idyllic surroundings of Conyers Farm. Limited to approximately 60 families, this 1,400-acre enclave features 10- to 20-acre homesites, a 100-acre lake, riding trails, polo and equestrian facilities, and tennis courts.* ABOVE: *The grand through-center entrance hall includes a delightful sitting area with one of the home's eight custom fireplaces. Also seen here are examples of the superior mouldings and woodwork on display throughout the interior.*

CHARACTERISTICS

Property size: 14 acres including 1,000 feet of frontage on Converse Lake.

Architectural style: Stone Tudor manor.

When built: 1986-1990.

Number of rooms: 18.

Distinctive features: Eight custom fireplaces, cherry paneling in the library, French doors and expansive windows overlooking lake views, walk-through art gallery, full-length loggia facing the lake, sky-lighted country kitchen, wine cellar, media room and private office.

Additional highlights: Private island included with property, extensive new landscaping amid older trees and plantings, and pool with step-down terrace. The 1,400-acre Conyers Farm community has indoor tennis, clubhouse, polo fields and riding trails, and is home to only 60 families.

A rocky ledge was blasted out before the foundation of reinforced concrete was poured. "After the interior walls were constructed," explains Stephen, "the shell was sealed and put through two heating seasons to allow for the inevitable settling and shrinkage prior to commencement of the plaster work." All interior and exterior walls—as well as every last window and door—were insulated for the utmost in energy efficiency. And finally came the low-maintenance systems, the elevator, wine cellar and eight fireplaces, along with the home's own art gallery, water-front loggia, walk-in closets, media room and more.

A computer and telecommunications wizard who has created new technology for the banking and brokerage community (and a man who builds yachts and has enjoyed offshore sailboat racing in his spare time), Stephen Nichols is justly proud of his accomplishments at Canaan Manor. "It's big but never overpowering, and a home where everyone has their special place. Mine is my office with the computer and easy chairs. My wife is happiest when it's Sunday afternoon, and she's all alone in the kitchen with her pots and pans preparing a crown roast or

OPPOSITE TOP: *With a total of 14 acres, much of it wooded, Canaan Manor offers its owners exceptional seclusion and privacy. The closest house is approximately 900 feet away.*
OPPOSITE BOTTOM: *In addition to 1,000 feet of frontage on Converse Lake, this estate comes with a private island.*
ABOVE: *Cozy and inviting, the master sitting area focuses on a large semi-circular window which affords lovely views of the lake.*

a duck for dinner. And my 16-year-old daughter has found her spot amid overstuffed pillows in the cupola." Occasionally they all get together for a paddle around the lake, rumored to have the best fishing around for large-mouth bass.

Limited to a mere 60 or so estate parcels, the surroundings of Conyers Farm have proven to be a very fitting address for the home of Stephen and Margaret Nichols. It's posh enough for championship polo, Geoffrey Kent-style (he and his wife, Jorie, were the first to build a home here); it's as treasured a find as a cozy cabin in the woods; and, as Stephen points out, "It's not really a neighborhood at all...the closest house to us is about 900 feet away." In a setting of special privilege and abundant natural beauty, this is a home that, like its surroundings, has been created without compromise.

Photography by Billy Black.

Canaan Manor was presented in Unique Homes by Jean Ruggerio, William Pitt Real Estate, Greenwich, CT.

Overbrook Farm

— *Stamford, Connecticut* —

Occupied and enjoyed by three generations of the same family since it was built more than 60 years ago, Overbrook Farm epitomizes the classic Connecticut country place. It's a stone's throw from Wall Street, but as far removed from the demands of city life as one could ever hope to be. Horseback riding and pigeon racing are remembered as favorite boyhood pastimes of Overbrook's present owner, an investment banker from Manhattan. He also recalls with fondness no less than half a dozen weddings which have been hosted on the grounds, and the printing press his father ran out back—a hobby now shared by his son.

Bordering 1,000 feet on the east branch of the Mianus River, the farm spreads out across 29 back country acres where woods and lawns are interspersed with English perennial gardens, mature oaks and pines, Japanese maples and flowering dogwoods. It's as pristine as an English park, but with many more delights: the charming riverside studio added in 1940 by Edward Durrel Stone, a converted barn ideal for casual dances, the nine-stall stable, greenhouse with potting room, caretaker's house and more. Over the years, each family member has had a special place at Overbrook to retreat

ABOVE & RIGHT:
Overbrook Farm's main residence is a Dutch Colonial home, circa 1929, designed by noted architect Richard Dana.
OPPOSITE TOP:
French doors open the formal dining room to the adjoining terrace.
OPPOSITE BOTTOM:
Brought from Bath, England, and added to the house in 1935, the library features 18th century paneling carved by the same artisan who created Avon's Badminton House.

to, whether indoors or out.

Encircled by native stone walls and flagstone terraces, the residence itself is a grand-scale Dutch Colonial, 21 rooms in size (exclusive of the seven full and two half-baths) and delightful at every turn. French doors open onto flower-filled patios, and window seats overlook azaleas and thousands of daffodils each spring; less than ten feet from the crisp white clapboard facade, the river runs swiftly by.

Each room bespeaks a comfortable dignity, from the bright tile-floored solarium to the formal living and dining rooms, warmed by two of the home's four fireplaces. Most spectacular of all, though, is the library dismantled in Bath, England, and reinstalled at Overbrook Farm in 1935. This superb mid-18th century room, all knotty pine and over 800 square feet in size, is attributed to the same artisan who created the celebrated Badminton

ABOVE: *Flowing virtually right outside the windows of the main residence, the east branch of the Mianus River is a wonderful complement to the idyllic acreage comprising Overbrook Farm.*

House located in Avon. The vast bookcases were a must for the original owner, who established an extensive collection of his favorite books as well as editions he personally printed here a generation ago. On the grounds, a printing press building, including a pressroom and private office with fireplace, still remains.

The owners have painstakingly preserved the essence of Overbrook, a genteel family home offering the kind of warmth and welcome that only age can foster; and at the same time, they have made it very much a part of their modern lives. It's the type of place successive generations look forward to calling "home."

Photography by Bud Trenka.

Overbrook Farm was presented in Unique Homes by Juner Properties, Stamford, CT, and LandVest, New Canaan, CT.

LEFT: *The farm's cow barn has been converted to a recreational building complete with two bowling lanes and a dance hall.* BELOW LEFT: *The estate features approximately 1,000 feet of river frontage.* BELOW: *The large in-ground pool.* BOTTOM: *At the water's edge is a quaint stone shed.*

CHARACTERISTICS

Property size: 29± acres, including 1,000 feet of frontage on the Mianus River's east branch.
Architectural style: Dutch Colonial.
When built: Circa 1929, with an addition in 1935 and renovations in the late 1980s.
Number of rooms: 21.
Outbuildings: "River House" (includes living room, kitchenette, bedroom and bath), converted barn with bowling lanes and dance hall, nine-stall stable with apartment overhead, chicken coops, greenhouse, caretaker's residence, nine-car garage complete with staff apartments, and a building which houses the owner's printing press and office.
Distinctive features: Four fireplaces, French doors, hardwood floors and elegant woodwork. The exquisitely detailed library, with mid-18th century carvings, was brought from England and reassembled at Overbrook Farm in 1935.

Windjammer Farm

North Salem, New York

"From the onset, this was meant to be a proper country house, with no overtones of stuffiness. I wanted a house where one felt a true sense of stepping back in time, a place of real romance and magic." Interior decorator Tyler Tinsworth's home in North Salem lives up to her words in a post-modern shingle design that for some resembles an old sea captain's cottage; for others it's a glimpse of the Tuscany countryside.

The hilly terrain, 50 miles north of New York City, was left virtually unchanged when Tyler and her husband, Stephen Weiss, embarked on Windjammer Farm

OPPOSITE TOP: *Designed by award-winning architects Shope, Reno and Wharton, Windjammer Farm is a stunning post-modern interpretation of the shingle style.* OPPOSITE BOTTOM: *Decorative fencing and expansive views beautifully set off the outdoor pool area.* ABOVE: *Three years in the making, this country manor encompasses some 10,000 square feet of living space. The numerous windows of the home and its open hilltop setting combine to afford long-range views from throughout the interior.*

eight years ago. From 1984 to 1987, the 10,000-square-foot house evolved under the award-winning architectural team of Shope, Reno and Wharton of Greenwich, Connecticut; and under Tinsworth herself, who insisted on a certain level of restraint.

"We wanted one central staircase, for instance; not a second back stairs and all the connotations that go with it," she says.

In addition to her design business, Tyler works with

OPPOSITE TOP: *A curved ceiling with distinctive skylight and a custom fireplace (one of five in the home) characterize the family room.* OPPOSITE BOTTOM LEFT: *French doors open the living room out to the wraparound terrace.* OPPOSITE BOTTOM RIGHT: *A window bay permits countryside views from the master bath Jacuzzi.* LEFT: *An abundance of windows allows "her" library to be bathed in natural light.* BOTTOM LEFT: *Special marble and distinctive fixtures were imported for the master bath.* BOTTOM RIGHT: *The family room and kitchen combine to form one expansive living area.*

Stephen in a real estate investment company. The demands of their professional lives, coupled with the activities of their children and step-children, necessitate living in a home that is highly functional and adaptable, but above all, nurturing. When they're all together and its a family dinner for a dozen or more, there's room in the kitchen for everyone to help themselves, sit at the table, or take their plate to the fireside. The fireplace in the kitchen/family room is one of five in the home, each

uniquely designed by the architect. Another Shope, Reno and Wharton hallmark is a dominant newel post at the base of the staircase, incorporating a latticework inset that echoes the expanse of multi-paned windows.

In addition to being a hunt master in North Salem, Stephen Weiss is an avid sailor, as are two of the children. "Windjammer seemed an appropriate name," says Tyler. "It was also the name of my daughter's first pony."

CHARACTERISTICS

Property size: 17+ acres.

Architectural style: Post-modern shingle.

Number or rooms: 14 (in main house).

Square footage: Approximately 10,000 square feet.

Number or bedrooms: Five (in main house).

Number of bathrooms: Seven (in main house).

Outbuildings: Three-car garage/two-bedroom, two-bath guest house.

Special features: Five custom fireplaces, skylights, French doors, floor-to-ceiling windows, custom European tile in baths, magnificent veranda off living and dining rooms, indoor and outdoor pools, computer room and children's library.

OPPOSITE TOP: *The formal dining room offers generous proportions and a fireplace with marble surround.* OPPOSITE BOTTOM LEFT: *The library includes plenty of shelf space for books, photographs and family memorabilia.* OPPOSITE BOTTOM RIGHT: *One of five bedrooms in the main house.* TOP LEFT: *Dressing areas in the master suite offer ample closet and storage space.* TOP RIGHT: *Windjammer Farm's entry hall.* ABOVE: *An enormous window wall creates a panoramic backrop for the master bedroom.* LEFT: *Classic tile work adorns the indoor pool area.*

And, while not a "farm" in the truest sense of the word, the property's 17 acres do include beautiful fields and hills, verdant lawns sloping down to the pool, and a separate three-car garage with guest/staff quarters. At the main entrance, a secluded inner courtyard keeps comings and goings private. It's also a place where the kids can play lacrosse.

Creating a home where the children and their friends would feel welcome in any room was perhaps Stephen and Tyler's foremost consideration. "I wanted every room to be used, and if the children felt like spreading out in the living room to do their homework, so much the better," Tyler maintains. "Nothing is off-limits here."

Regardless of where you are in the house, sunshine is ever-present. The living and dining rooms open through French doors to a wraparound terrace. Skylights projecting from the curved family room ceil-

ABOVE: *The center island kitchen features double sinks, double wall ovens, a British Aga stove, a cooktop, custom ash cabinetry and a large butler's pantry/wet bar.* RIGHT: *The sitting room in the master suite has a fireplace and windows on three sides.*

RIGHT: *With its lovely fireplace and terrace access, the spacious living room is ideal for entertaining.*
BELOW: *The trophy room is a warm and inviting space complete with built-in shelves and a fireplace.*

ing flood the room with warmth. The sitting room is banked by windows on three exposures. And the master bath has its own sunny bay by day and a view to the stars at night.

In what they consider the most wonderfully rural part of Westchester County, Tyler Tinsworth and Stephen Weiss have built a house that is relevant to the needs of today, yet conversant with history. All the wonders of the modern world are here, including an indoor pool, a computer room and a kitchen that Tyler proudly admits "is perfection." There remain, however, many inescapable links to the past: a trophy room filled with family treasures, bathrooms detailed in custom European tiles, terra cotta pots filled with the blossoms of summer, and the laughter of children. It's a harmony that often takes a lifetime to achieve.

Photography by Bob Vergara.

Windjammer Farm was presented in Unique Homes by Portfolio Properties, Greenwich, CT.

RIGHT: *Restored to its original magnificence, the library sets a formal tone with its paneled walls stained in a rich mahogany finish, carved plaster ceiling treatment and imposing marble fireplace.* OPPOSITE TOP: *The front facade of the residence.* OPPOSITE BOTTOM: *The home enjoys lovely views overlooking Tuxedo Lake, one of three bodies of water in Tuxedo Park.*

La Falaise

Tuxedo Park, New York

The name given to this estate means "the cliff," but in fact there are several ridges making a steep, leafy descent from the house down to Tuxedo Lake. This sparkling body of water is one of three in the 2,500-acre enclave Pierre Lorillard IV carved out more than a century ago beneath the Ramapo Mountains. What he envisioned was the elite retreat for New Yorkers, where hunting and socializing with one's own kind was de rigueur, and where the finest examples of American domestic architecture would be occupied by Astors, Pells, Mortimers, and the like. Emily Post, daughter of Tuxedo Park's co-designer Bruce Price, found much inspiration for her essentials of etiquette while growing up here. Bridge, tennis and golf were all pioneered in the

Property size: Nearly four acres overlooking Tuxedo Lake.
Architectural style: Tudor Revival.
Number of rooms: 13+.
Square footage: 10,000.
Number of bedrooms: Six (not including six staff bedrooms in main house).
Outbuildings: New oversized four-car garage, designed in the style of the main house, and featuring a 2,000-square-foot apartment above.
Distinctive features: Original leaded and stained glass windows, many hand-carved fireplace mantels, fireplaces in all principal rooms plus two in master suite (one in bedroom, one in master library), grand spiral staircase, intricate mouldings, carved plaster ceilings, priceless chandeliers and sconces, large third-floor guest suite suitable for conversion to playrooms or office/studio.
Additional highlights: The estate is in mint condition and has expansive views over Tuxedo Lake, the centerpiece of a century-old enclave comprising three lakes, 2,500 acres of wooded parkland and panoramas of the Ramapo Mountains—all less than an hour's drive from New York City.

Park by Americans in the late 1800s, as was the modern-day version of "black tie." At the first Autumn Ball in 1886, Lorillard's son arrived in a short dinner jacket, without the tails, and the term "tuxedo" caught on quickly.

Tuxedo Park celebrated its centennial a few years back, and now it's time for a similar party at La Falaise, a grand old place which has seen as many alterations to its Tudor Revival design as it has owners. The exterior is as Tudor as it is Victorian as it is Colonial, but indoors, it's all classic Georgian, except for the Edwardian library with a magnificent fireplace of soft marble. Over the past four years, a young Wall Street investment banker and his wife have redone virtually the entire house, spending three months alone on the library, where every inch of

wall surface was stripped to reveal the original wood-work, now stained in a rich mahogany finish.

The original 100-year-old leaded and stained glass windows, French doors and eight fireplaces remain, and there are still the stone steps on the lakeside entrance where horse-drawn buggies once made their approach. "But we literally had to create a new entrance on the opposite side of the house, and that meant rebuilding the foyer, and then we needed a functional kitchen, all new bathrooms, the carriage house..." and so continues the wife, mother and general contractor at La Falaise.

She says she made all her mistakes in the living room, the first space to be redone. Though judging by the exquisite renovation throughout, all the decisions were the right ones, from relocating the dining room to a grand-scale space full of windows overlooking the lake and woodlands, to bringing flower-filled fabrics and fresh colors to rooms that were once painted in pale mint green.

"The place was really a wreck when we came here,

but it had this positive aura. It hugs you. Others who have stayed here say the same thing. When we're away I know the house is sad. It needs people and parties and children. And we've certainly given it that!" A few years back this lady was number crunching on Wall Street and coming home at night to a one-bedroom apartment in Manhattan. A husband, a house in Tuxedo Park and three babies later, she seems quite amenable to the life here, described by Emily Post in 1911 as follows: "A place where a man who has to work in New York City may live the year round, where there is the highest altitude for the least number of miles from town, a place where little children may be allowed to run at large in safety—in other words, as a beautiful place of perma-nent homes, Tuxedo Park is as nearly ideal as can be found."

Photography by James Pearson.

La Falaise was presented in Unique Homes by Cindy B. Van Schaack, Towne & Country Properties, Tuxedo Park, NY.

OPPOSITE: *The master suite includes a gracious bedroom and an adjoining master library. Both rooms are appointed with wood-burning fireplaces.* LEFT: *The kitchen was redesigned and outfitted to be totally functional for everything from small family dinners to grand-scale entertaining.* BELOW: *Moved to its current location as part of the home's extensive renovation, the formal dining room now occupies a light, spacious area with picture window views of Tuxedo Lake and the surrounding woodlands.*

Brookside

Rye, New York

Through ornamental iron gates a winding paved drive sweeps along manicured lawns, age-old evergreens and leafy arbors. Rising in the distance is the noble Georgian mansion, its symmetry articulated in bright white shutters, towering chimneys, arched dormers and a shady porte cochere. Inside, a world of age-old privilege unfolds; since its creation 80 years ago, Brookside has been one of the most distinguished estates in America.

Originally, the mansion built by the Greer family occupied 88 acres of fields and woodlands in southern Westchester County. The Greers lived in the home for some 30 years, after which time it was purchased by Miss Jean Flagler, on the occasion of her marriage to Mark Matthews. It was a fine wedding gift indeed: a 32-room residence of museum-quality detail, its interiors displaying some of the finest workmanship of the 20th century, and its lush surrounds embraced by sweeping terraces, formal gardens and the quiet beauty of the countryside.

LEFT: *The full-length portico affords an exceptional vantage point for surveying the estate's beautifully landscaped grounds.*
ABOVE: *As sturdy as it is imposing, this three-story Georgian Colonial mansion of approximately 20,000 square feet was built to be fireproof with steel-reinforced concrete base flooring, solid brick walls and a slate roof.*
OPPOSITE: *Just inside the ornamental iron front gates, the winding drive begins its approach past manicured lawns and stately trees to the porte cochere entry seen here.*

OPPOSITE TOP: *A trompe l'oeil ceiling and walls of multi-paned windows help create a light and airy ambience in the solarium.* OPPOSITE BOTTOM: *Brightly colored flower beds, lush lawns and large expanses of flagstone terracing surround the estate's two pools (one for adults, one for children). A delightful gazebo built out of wrought iron occupies the area between these pools.* LEFT: *Panoramic views overlooking the rear grounds complement casual dining on the terrace.* BELOW: *The quality of the restoration carried out by the present owners is immediately evident upon entering the grand reception hall. Here, the handsome mouldings and curving staircase only hint at the refined sophistication that pervades the entire house.*

Named for the rushing brook that meanders through the property, Brookside was sold after Mrs. Matthews' death to its third and present owners. The estate now encompasses a more manageable 24 acres, though it remains well secluded, enviably private and still one of the largest and most beautiful properties in the county.

Over the past decade, the 20,000-square-foot residence has been revived and restored to perfection, and the patina the home had acquired over the years is now more glowing than ever. Herringbone parquet floors are at home amid fine paintings and period antiques. A solarium that is all white wicker and sunshine brings year-round gardens into the home. A dining room befitting state dinners shimmers amid mirrors, candlelight and crystal. No room is without a host of magnificent fittings, from windows swathed in silk in the living room,

to the finely carved mantelpiece and paneling in the executive library.

While the home shares an inescapable affinity with the past, its owners have seen to a host of contemporary requirements, among them an all-new kitchen and butler's pantry on the first floor. On the second floor, another kitchen and a breakfast room are convenient to five bedroom suites (each with fireplace). Also on this level are exercise and sitting rooms adjoining the master suite, plus an assortment of staff rooms. The top floor has additional bedrooms suited for children and/or staff, and on

the lower level there is a playroom plus a wine cellar and darkroom.

For all its interior finery, from the 12 exquisite fireplaces to the faux-finished columns, Brookside derives its grand-scale beauty from a setting that would hardly be possible to duplicate today. The immediate residential grounds encompass five acres of velvety lawns, trim evergreens and an endless variety of specimen trees and plantings. From a broad full-length portico, wide steps extend down to a swimming pool with gazebo, a smaller children's pool and an all-weather tennis court. Natural

OPPOSITE: *The paneled family library offers a host of classic appointments including finely crafted mouldings and woodwork and a carved wood fireplace.* LEFT: *Also on the main level is an executive office. This private retreat sets a formal tone with its rich cabinetry, paneled walls and large fireplace. A powder room adjoins this space.* BELOW: *The spacious living room includes an ornate fireplace and double French doors which access the solarium.*

CHARACTERISTICS

Property size: 24 acres.

Architectural style: Georgian.

When built: 1911 to 1913. Meticulously restored in the 1980s.

Number of rooms: 32.

Square footage: Approximately 20,000.

Number of bedrooms: 10 (not including staff quarters).

Number of baths: 10½.

Outbuildings: Two-story, four-bedroom brick caretaker's residence overlooking a pond; two garages (one attached).

Distinctive features: Columned porte cochere entry and broad full-length brick portico, superb paneling, carved fireplaces and herringbone-patterned floors. Also, there are beautiful fittings and fixtures of marble and crystal, fireplaces in every principal room as well as all five bedrooms on the second floor. There are two kitchens, a full-length sun room off the master suite, a wine cellar and photo darkroom on the lower level.

Additional highlights: Two swimming pools (one for children), private orchard, gazebo, tennis court and running brook. Up to 20 acres of green, open land suitable for sporting field or subdivision. Prime location in southern Westchester County, only 35 minutes from midtown Manhattan.

rock outcroppings rise to rolling hills, and walled formal gardens oversee the placid waters of the reflecting pool. A wooded boundary surrounds the remaining 20 level acres known as Brookside Park. This parcel offers a variety of possibilities and would convert well to a private golf course or polo field.

Since its completion in 1913, only three families have lived at Brookside, and while each has brought an individual style to the home, they've all seemed to share in the notion that history is worth repeating. It is a place of permanence, completeness and lasting design that doubtlessly will continue to age well in the generations to come.

Photography by Lorna McIntyre Studio.

Brookside was presented in Unique Homes by John T. Henningsen, Inc., Real Estate, Rye, NY.

OPPOSITE TOP: *Thanks to the current owner's renovation efforts, the kitchen is now a state-of-the-art facility complete with butler's pantry.* OPPOSITE BOTTOM: *The luxurious master bedroom adjoins a sunny sitting room.* LEFT: *Also included in the master suite are "his" and "her" dressing rooms. Shown here is "her" dressing room, a lavish area with marble fireplace and bath.* ABOVE: *Large enough for a banquet, the formal dining room is appointed with hand-painted wall coverings, wainscoting and a fireplace. A separate family dining room is also featured in the main-floor layout.*

Executive Privilege
on a Landmark Block

New York City

From the outside, where the wrought iron grille on the entry doors is neatly flanked by columns supporting the balustrade and balcony above, it appears to be one of those Upper East Side houses that's been around forever. Nowhere does it say "By Appointment Only," but one clearly has the impression that an invitation to 116 East 65th Street is required. It's one of five original townhouses attributed to Stanford White on this landmark block between Park and Lexington Avenues, and one of the few mansions in town that still boasts the great proportions of its century-old design.

Inside, one has the option of exploring the townhouse via either elevator or a central skylighted staircase. Take the stairs. You'll get a better perspective on the dramatic 13-foot ceilings, the sunlight that filters down into the home on every level, the music that travels from parlor to bedroom and beyond. You can't help but be impressed by the property's overall 100-foot flow from front to back: tall windows facing north streetside, lush garden terraces to the south, and, in-between, a home that has recently undergone a multi-million-dollar

RIGHT: *Shown here is the handsome entry facade at 116 East 65th Street. The house is one of three on the block that are attributed to Stanford White.*
OPPOSITE TOP: *The stately living room includes a classic marble fireplace and French doors to a small balcony overlooking the street.*
OPPOSITE MIDDLE: *Pocket doors open from the center landing to the formal dining room, featuring a fireplace and beamed ceiling.*
OPPOSITE BOTTOM: *A spiral staircase leads from the second-floor terrace down to the landscaped garden area.*

renovation to provide the ultimate residential and corporate address in Manhattan.

This 8,400-square-foot house gives new meaning to the concept of "turnkey," as it comes with much more than the usual furnishings, silver and dishes. Scanning the 27-page inventory you'll find 12 Chippendale dining room chairs, a pair of antique Chinese silk tapestries, alabaster lamps, 91-inch-high Venetian-style mirrors from England, custom needlepoint carpets, Berber rugs and runners, Dhurrie wall panels, petit point pillows, Onkyo stereo equipment and Fitz and Floyd china, as well as two copiers and laser jet printers...virtually everything needed so that the running of a worldwide business empire and world-class entertaining can all be accommodated under one roof.

The house—with its six levels of living space— is owned by a European executive whose global business can't stop when he comes to town, so the residence

has been ingeniously transformed to meet every last professional as well as personal obligation. This includes fully equipped offices on the main and lower levels. The owner's private library suite, occupying half of the fourth floor, is a sophisticated retreat painted in classic hunter green and complete with one of the home's eight working fireplaces, a full wet bar and adjoining bath and kitchen facilities.

When working day is done, evening festivities begin out in the brick-terraced garden amid rhododendrons and climbing ivy, or in the living room upstairs where French doors open to the front balcony. Pocket doors allow this parlor to be intimately closed off from the rest of the floor, or opened to a 60-foot expanse of entertaining space that includes the reception hall with its full-length caned settee and Indo-Oriental rug, and the formal dining room warmly appointed in mahogany and marquetry. Just beyond,

🏛

CHARACTERISTICS

Property size: 20' x 100' lot.
Architectural style: Brick townhouse attributed to Stanford White.
When built: Circa 1880s. Completely restored and updated.
Number of rooms: 20+.
Square footage: 8,400±.
Number of bedrooms: Four suites (plus staff accommodations).
Number of baths: Four full, three half-baths.
Distinctive features: Eight working fireplaces, fine mouldings and wainscoting, ceilings as high as 13 feet, balconies, central skylighted staircase, professional offices on main floor and lower level. Rear garden with fountain and perennial plantings. A completely turnkey address, with furnishings, equipment and all accessories, from copying machines to cookware.
Special amenities: Elevator, central air conditioning, high-tech security, 50-line phone capacity, complete cable service, pre-wired for Quotron, two full kitchens, kitchenette and wet bar in owner's private library/study, kitchenette on ground floor, Jacuzzi in marble master bath.
Additional highlights: One of three remaining townhouses attributed to Stanford White on its landmark block. Offered with many original fittings and completely restored, it is an ideal address for a world-class residence, embassy or corporate headquarters.

the gourmet kitchen leads onto an outdoor deck with a spiral staircase winding down to the garden. When it's a private visit with family and friends, the owner prefers to dine on the fifth floor, where a charming country kitchen opens to a bay-windowed garden room and an adjoining terrace equipped with running water and outdoor speakers.

Surely there are other private residences in the world that are as scrupulously planned and elegantly styled, but how many of them were built a century ago by a famous architect, are fully computerized, have fresh basil growing out back, and feature an address that's only two minutes on foot from Le Cirque?

Photography by Michael Merle.

This landmark townhouse was presented in Unique Homes by Jean-Marc Levet & Partners, New York, NY.

Fantasy Spa on Long Island

—— Upper Brookville, New York ——

ABOVE: *Dramatic architectural design and park-like grounds define this contemporary retreat.* OPPOSITE TOP: *The glass-enclosed pool and spa area affords an exotic ambience year-round.* OPPOSITE MIDDLE: *A freestanding fireplace and cathedral ceiling accentuate the spaciousness of the living room.* OPPOSITE BOTTOM: *A paddle court and game room are part of the magnificent indoor sports complex.*

This cedar and glass design by architect P. H. Tuan is a modern masterwork of hard-edge line and abounding light, with walls of windows rising to the treetops and embracing a view of waterfalls and woodlands. The nine-acre setting is a natural for quiet contemplation and active recreation. Much more than a residence, this home is a spa as well as a complete resort environment, one custom planned for keeping mind and body in top form.

Beyond the electronically controlled gates of this verdant compound, past the azure waters of the lagoon-shaped pool, the interior is sleek, white-washed and forever open to the outdoors. From a living space that is both embracing and endless, a glass corridor links the four-bedroom California contemporary residence to the adjoining spa amenities. First there is the 40-foot indoor pool, surrounded by glass and tropical gardens, with retractable window panels opening onto a gym. Here, the latest in workout equipment and a wet bar are accompanied by all the amenities one expects to find in a first-class health club, including an enormous sauna, changing rooms and baths.

There is a room for billiards and pinball, a lounge equipped with wide-screen TV and fireplace, a professional indoor paddle tennis court and even a viewing room for spectators. With 19,000 square feet of active living space and acres of outdoor seclusion, it's as welcome an escape as any from the pressures of modern life. And, when it's time for a workout of the mind, there are many places ideal for peaceful seclusion, including the home's own meditation room or the reflecting pools and exquisite Japanese gardens found out-of-doors.

Photography by Peter Margonelli (exterior) and Michael Forester (interiors).

This property was presented in Unique Homes by Coldwell Banker/Previews® Schlott Realtors®, Locust Valley, NY.

CHARACTERISTICS

Property size: Nine acres.

Architectural style: Cedar and glass California contemporary.

Square footage: 19,000.

Number of bedrooms: Four principal bedrooms plus guest suite and staff quarters.

Distinctive features: Ultra-sophisticated, high-tech design for an "at home" resort, with enclosed glass walkways linking recreation and living areas. Freestanding fireplace in the cathedral-ceilinged living room, fireplace also in the master suite.

Additional highlights: Grounds include a lagoon-style outdoor pool with waterfall, Japanese gardens, three reflecting pools and dense surrounding woodlands for privacy.

Crestley

Harding Township, New Jersey

During the American Revolution, the fields and farms of Harding Township supplied food and shelter to the troops of General George Washington. History is well remembered here in the national parklands at Jockey Hollow, site of Washington's winter encampment; and the township proudly maintains the Tempe Wick House as a historic museum. Today, this still rural and remote pocket of Morris County bespeaks the well-mannered ways of old money. Bridle trails and rushing streams cut through a landscape rich with untouched meadows and woodlands, while country homes of grand design and dimension stand tucked away at the end of private, winding lanes.

One of the community's largest and most beautiful intact estates is Crestley, a property spanning well over 80 acres of picturesque fields, woods and magnificently planned residential grounds. Located only 34 miles from Manhattan, the setting most closely resembles a private English park, complete with some 5,000 tulips and a wealth of flowering trees ready to herald the approach of

ABOVE: *A focal point of the main courtyard is a delightful tiled reflecting pool with fountain and stone wall.* RIGHT: *The view into the estate from the entry gates only hints at the scope of the residence that awaits at the end of the drive.* OPPOSITE: *The stone and brick facade, with its multi-paned windows and Yorkshire flag slate roof, would not be out of place in the English countryside.*

spring. Annuals, perennials and evergreens are everywhere; and as the days grow longer into summer, terraced patios and walkways welcome the warm weather with a host of areas for entertaining. In addition to a pond and small brooks that parallel two boundaries of the estate, the property features a magnificently designed Pugliese pool embraced by beautiful birches and a waterfall cascading down rocky outcroppings. Nearby are an entertainment cabana and illuminated tennis court.

Built in the 1920s, Crestley's stone and brick manor house is most closely associated with the Colonial style, though its great charm and character speak more of a mood than a distinct architectural period. Carved into a knoll with uninterrupted views all around, the home is brilliantly wedded to its surroundings. The splashing fountain in the main courtyard is easily heard from a side terrace. The enclosed porch, filled with sunshine and floral chintz, opens through walls of glass to the stone ter-

ABOVE: *The pool terrace is a popular gathering spot in the summer.* OPPOSITE—TOP LEFT: *A view across the grounds.* MIDDLE LEFT: *The tennis court is lighted for night play.* TOP RIGHT: *The formal living room.* MIDDLE RIGHT: *The banquet-size dining room.* BOTTOM: *The enclosed porch adjoins the stone terrace.*

race and gardens. The banquet-size dining room features an enormous bow window with a verdant view of green, and a deep front-to-back center hall provides natural light from foyers at both ends. Renovations undertaken in 1983 have transformed Crestley into a home of expansive warmth and comfort; a home that is impressive without ever being imposing.

One of the privileges of owning a property such as this is the opportunity to enjoy an active professional life in the city while being able to come home to the quiet pleasures of the country each night. It is a measure of rare success, and one of a family's great rewards.

Photography by George E. Peirce, Studio 84.

Crestley was presented in Unique Homes by Molly Mackenzie Tonero, Capital Properties Group, a Division of Weichert, Realtors, Morris Plains, NJ.

CHARACTERISTICS

Property size: 81+ acres.

Architectural style: Stone and brick Colonial.

When built: 1920s, with renovations in the 1980s.

Number of rooms: 19.

Number of bedrooms: 11.

Number of baths: Eight full, four half-baths.

Outbuildings: Two-bedroom caretaker's cottage, barn, pool house and garage.

Distinctive features: Exquisite mouldings and paneling, seven working fireplaces, Yorkshire flag slate roof, Jacuzzi spas in three of the baths, lower level with game room, bar and exercise room. Totally updated mechanical, plumbing and electrical systems.

Additional highlights: One of the area's largest intact estates. Within an hour of Manhattan.

Stonewall

Washington, D.C.

"**E**ssentially, it was a big, dowdy old Washington house; the kind you see all over the place here," states architect James D. Wilner. "It had all the elements of great design, but lacked the flow. And, it didn't relate to its surroundings at all." Get him started and Wilner will go on and on about the old homes of northwest Washington, D.C.; homes that he says are usually stone or brick, typically with a formal center hall design and all too often restricted in their openness. "The problem with stone," he elaborates, "is that you can't create any larger openings. You start carving away and soon the whole structure is in jeopardy."

A little over a year ago, Jim Wilner stopped complaining and started reconfiguring the house at 2700 Upton Street for a client who gave him free reign on everything except the budget. In addressing the project, Wilner said he merely had to answer the question, "What does the house need to fulfill its own sense of spirit?"

The solution was one great room—the centerpiece of an addition to be placed smack-dab in the middle of the rear elevation and reaching far into the lofty views over Rock Creek Park. "You have to respect the existing house," explains Wilner, "and here, the Georgian center hall layout allowed this openness to happen." Whereas the foyer was once the common thread for the flanking

CHARACTERISTICS

Property size: Three-quarters of an acre.
Architectural style: Center-hall stone Colonial manor.
When built: 1922. Totally renovated in 1991.
Number of bedrooms: Four, plus two-bedroom apartment on lower level.
Number of baths: Five and one-half, plus full bath in apartment.
Distinctive features: Original doors and hardware (restored), eight-foot-tall French doors opening to balconies and terraces, original coffered ceiling in solarium, original marble mantel in library, 18-foot ceilings in Grand Salon, media room with bar, game room opening to terraces and gardens, self-contained two-bedroom apartment, and master suite with fireplace, sitting area and private roof terrace.
Additional highlights: Stonewall is set high on a hill in the heart of the city, with superb views of Rock Creek Park. It was the winner of the 1992 ADAC Design of the Year award.

public areas, each space now has an expanded focus in the newly added great room, where roof beams are raised 18 feet high, the sunshine pours in through enormous windows on three sides, and semi-circular decks soften the lines of the 24-foot-deep extension.

While the renovation of this 1922 residence neighboring the home of Senator George McGovern and the late Marjorie Merriweather Post's "Hillwood" has brought a contemporary flair to the floor plan, there is still a sense of the period when the home served as an important host to Washington society. In the library, one finds the original marble mantel and connecting balcony. The stone wall in the solarium remains, as it has for some 70 years, beneath a beautiful coffered ceiling. And, in the master suite, it's the best of both worlds as the owners enjoy 45 feet of linear hanging closet space, a

master bath with whirlpool tub, and French doors opening to a wisteria-covered arbor over the roof terrace.

Before any wall was opened, before any bleached floorboard or granite countertop was laid, the architect's first consideration was the setting, for the home has always had a wonderful sense of place. The balconies and terraces overlook English gardens and winding stone pathways. The parterres of English boxwood and the reflecting pool are charming and intimate; the park views are broad and wildly lush. Like the house itself, the surroundings offer a rich display of contrasts. Some are serene; some are surprising. Yet, they all seem to belong.

Photography by Bill Lyons.

Stonewall was presented in Unique Homes by Ellen Wilner, Re/Max 2000 Realtors, North Bethesda, MD.

OPPOSITE: **Stonewall's 1991 addition adds a contemporary flair to the classic stone facade.**
ABOVE: **Housed in this new addition is the Grand Salon, which features an 18-foot ceiling, faux-wood paneling, walls of glass and balconies overlooking Rock Creek Park.**

Penderyn

Cheston-on-Wye, Eastern Shore of Maryland

"When we first bought the land, there were just clammers along the waterfront," reminisces Mario Boiardi about the Eastern Shore peninsula he purchased in 1984. "After that, it was quite another story!" Over the next four and one-half years, these 44 acres situated at a picturesque confluence of the Wye River, DeCoursey Cove and the Wye Narrows would become the talk of Queen Anne's County as the Boiardis created one of the most outstanding Georgian homes ever built. Sailors, fishermen and speed boaters still stop in their wakes to take in the vista that includes stately courts of London pavers, masonry of handmade rose-colored brick, Palladian windows atop French doors, and a pool house far grander in style or scope than most private residences; in all, some 25,000 square feet of pure Georgian design.

A self-described Anglophile with a passion for the symmetry and majesty of Georgian architecture, Mr.

OPPOSITE TOP: *The oak-paneled billiard room has virtually invisible secret wall compartments.* OPPOSITE BOTTOM: *An English Perry chandelier, circa 1840, is a focal point of the formal dining room.* ABOVE: *Penderyn's facade displays handmade bricks, English chimney pots atop corbelled chimneys, and custom Palladian windows and French doors.* LEFT: *The 157-foot dock has 11 slips plus water and electric service.*

LEFT: *The 35' x 50' heated swimming pool is enhanced by side platforms with whirlpool jets and a diving depth of 10 feet.* BELOW: *The gallery is a majestic corridor linking the sweeping two-story marble foyer with the formal drawing room. Matched crystal lanterns illuminate the artisan-plastered quoin vault ceiling.*

Boiardi explained how he ended up with a home of such proportions. "It's quite simple. If we extended the structure in one direction, we had to match it on the opposing side." That's just the way it is with Georgians; beauty from balance, purity from precision. One advantageous concession was to bisect the rectangular layout with a long marble gallery from front to back, bringing in the beautiful water views and, through a series of archways beneath a quoin vault ceiling, linking the family living and dining rooms to the Great Court.

With over a mile of waterfront, there is scarcely a room without a view of blue; and for Mario Boiardi,

this aspect was as essential as any antique or Impressionist painting he and his wife Maureen have purchased for Penderyn. "For me, looking at water is like looking into a fire...mesmerizing and always changing." Though he claims not to be much of a boating expert, Mr. Boiardi has outfitted the property with a 157-foot dock providing 11 slips, fresh water and electricity—an appropriate mooring for ocean-bound yachts.

For the Boiardis, the home truly succeeds in its flexibility. It can be host to the grandest of galas amidst fluted white columns with gilded Corinthian capitals, handmade banisters and doors of solid mahogany, antique English lanterns and chandeliers, and superb Regency furnishings. It can be homey, particularly in the family rooms that are decidedly French country with rough plaster walls and flower-filled fabrics. When summer comes, it's casual as can be at poolside and in the pool house, with its sauna, fitness room and bar. And, when a winter chill rides in from the shore, 11 fireplaces—marble, pine and limestone, most from the 18th and 19th centuries—glow with Penderyn's inescapable warmth.

ABOVE: **A 17th century French limestone fireplace is the centerpiece of the living room, which includes an informal dining area and pool terrace access.** OPPOSITE TOP: **The library is an elegant retreat with its hand-painted silk wallpaper and late 18th century carved pine Chippendale fireplace.** OPPOSITE BOTTOM: **The pool house provides two large changing rooms with showers, sauna, sitting room, wet bar, refrigerator, ice maker and a spiral staircase to a mirrored mezzanine fitness room.**

In a house of such dimension, it is rare to feel so at home, and much can be learned from the Boiardis' intelligent and energetic sense of style. Maureen scoured Europe for all the magnificent furnishings, then came home to plant thousands of flowering bulbs on the lawns. Mario, while overseeing the entire project, took a special interest in creating the perfect kitchen. (He is the son of the gentleman who created the Chef Boyardee empire.) Faux-finish artist Helen Hobbs, Maureen's daughter, worked up a palette of jubilant tones for the walls, and Amish carpenters were employed for the paneling. The very faithful and appropriate Regency interiors were the result of a tight collaboration between the owners and interior designer Bernice Cavallo and her husband, Stefan, son of the revered S. Cavallo of New York.

The overall effect is inviting and never overwhelming, highly personal yet never imposed. Penderyn is a home that speaks well of its creators.

Photography by Richard Walker.

Penderyn was presented in Unique Homes by Shirley A. Mueller, Uncommon Properties Inc., New York, NY.

CHARACTERISTICS

Property size: 44 acres.

Architectural style: Authentic re-creation of a Georgian manor.

When built: 1985-1989.

Number of rooms: 32.

Square footage: 25,000 square feet.

Outbuildings: Screened summerhouse, pool house, garage.

Special features: Museum-quality lighting, 20-line phone system, two kitchenettes in addition to the main kitchen, 50-foot swimming pool, fitness center and sauna in the pool house.

Additional highlights: One mile of direct waterfront, English formal gardens, 11-slip dock, duck blind, stately courts and terraces.

Mirador

In the Autumn Light of the Blue Ridge Mountains

— Albemarle County, Virginia —

Like many an old Southern tale, the story of Mirador begins with the land itself, where the Greenwood Valley starts its gentle rise to the Blue Ridge, and only occasionally is the stillness broken in a galloping rush of hounds and horns and red hunting coats. The first to make his home on the spot now known as Mirador was Colonel James M. Bowen, who acquired the land granted to his grandfather for service in the French and Indian War. The original square brick house was built in 1832, and the Colonel positioned it well to capture the endless Piedmont views. He christened his home "El Mirador"; with the panorama scarcely changed today, the name is still quite fitting.

After being passed on to the Colonel's daughter, Mary, the estate was eventually conveyed in 1892 to Colonel Chiswell ("Chillie") Dabney Langhorne, a kind Virginia gentleman who was once described as "the handsomest and most likeable man of the Old Dominion." In order to accommodate his eight children, "Charming Charlie" added two brick wings onto the original Bowen house. Though he intended to occupy Mirador only in summer, Langhorne retired at the age of 60, sold his house in Richmond and moved everyone to Mirador. Prior to this time, it is rumored that he sent his family away each fall so that he could entertain his men friends with much quail shooting and poker playing.

During the Langhornes' time here, life was centered around riding, fox hunting and an endless parade of guests. The five Langhorne daughters, often considered the last of the great Virginia belles, were responsible for

OPPOSITE BOTTOM: *Since the days when the Langhorne boys shot bullfrogs on the pond, this scenic spot has refreshed grazing cows and picnickers alike.*
ABOVE: *Nestled in the Greenwood Valley, Mirador is one of the South's finest country estates. Today, the 19-room Georgian brick mansion commands 375 acres of terraced lawns, landscaped gardens and rich farmland—all set against the panoramic Blue Ridge Mountains.*
LEFT: *Mirador is rich in daily scenes of pastoral beauty.*

a constant stream of suitors at Mirador. Irene was so beautiful, it is said she received 60 proposals of marriage before she finally settled on artist Charles Dana Gibson, whose drawings of his wife and her sisters immortalized the "Gibson Girls."

Daughter Nancy became better known as Lady Astor, wife of Waldorf Astor and the first female member to take her seat as a member of British Parliament. Quick-witted and controversial, she once said to Winston Churchill, "If you were my husband, I would put poison in your coffee."

"Nancy," he replied, "if you were my wife, I'd drink it."

TOP: *Mirador's front facade.* ABOVE LEFT: *Entrance to one of the many roads that wind throughout the estate.* ABOVE RIGHT: *Viewed from the front drive, the stately home still welcomes visitors as it has since 1832.* OPPOSITE TOP: *The Virginia Historic Landmark sign designating Mirador as the childhood home of Lady Astor.* OPPOSITE MIDDLE: *Complementing the main house are the gardens, rich in architectural detail. The colonnade at the rear of the house has seen many a festive garden party.* OPPOSITE BOTTOM: *The serpentine walls which flank green walkways are patterned after a design by Thomas Jefferson.*

MIRADOR

THIS WAS THE GIRLHOOD HOME OF
VISCOUNTESS NANCY ASTOR, FIRST
WOMAN MEMBER OF THE BRITISH
PARLIAMENT. SHE WAS A DAUGHTER
OF CHISWELL DABNEY LANGHORNE,
WHO BOUGHT "MIRADOR" IN 1892.
THE HOUSE WAS BUILT SOMETIME
AFTER 1832 FOR JAMES M. BOWEN.
1961

CHARACTERISTICS

Property size: 375 acres.

Architectural style: Brick Georgian.

When built: 1832; modernized and enlarged in the 1930s; refurbished again in the 1980s.

Number of rooms: 19.

Number of bedrooms: Eight.

Number of baths: Seven and one-half.

Outbuildings: A total of 16 including main barn complex, six cottages, brick stables and garages.

Distinctive features: Adam mantels, 14 fireplaces, French doors, corbeled cornices, hand-painted Chinese wall coverings, Chippendale mouldings, herringbone parquet floors, walnut paneling, marble-floored rotunda-style foyer with freestanding circular staircase. "English basement" with staff quarters, game room and orchid house. Exquisite period rooms on upper floors, extensive terrace and porch areas, swimming pool, tennis court, indoor sports complex, two small lakes, colorful gardens and productive farmland.

Additional highlights: Located 17 miles west of Charlottesville. The childhood home of Lady Astor (Nancy) and Irene Langhorne, the original "Gibson Girl," Mirador is one of the finest older estates in historic Albemarle County. The property boasts superb Georgian architecture, excellent facilities for a cattle/horse operation, and stunning views of the Blue Ridge Mountains.

Other Langhorne ladies included Phyllis, who built the brick stable opposite the south facade of the main residence, and Mrs. Ronald Tree, the Colonel's granddaughter, who with her husband upgraded and further enlarged the manor and gardens. Subsequent owners of the estate since 1950 have refurbished the outbuildings and returned Mirador to the farming operation that began here more than 150 years ago.

Today, the 19-room brick Georgian stands amid 375 acres of terraced lawns, landscaped gardens and rich farmland. The scent of lilacs wafts through French doors, into the paneled dining room, where a corbeled cornice

RIGHT & BELOW: *A fitting introduction to the classic detail of the home is offered by the circular entrance hall, featuring a curving freestanding staircase and a marble floor with inlaid marble and bronze compass. There is no more dramatic view at Mirador than straight up the stairway to the leaded glass skylight on the second floor.*
BOTTOM: *On the second floor are four bedrooms, one of which is said to be haunted by the ghost of Mrs. Bowen, the wife of Mirador's first owner.*

and marble mantel crafted by the Brothers Adam are among the embellishments. In the firelight of the walnut library, guests linger long after dinner, reading the guest book filled with names of visitors to Mirador, among them Henry Ford, Marshall Field and Lord Halifax. Brick serpentine walls wind in Jeffersonian fashion through walkways and gardens. Just beyond, where the young Langhorne boys used to shoot bullfrogs on the pond, the water reflects the grazing cattle and leafy hills. And, in one of the four bedrooms on the second floor of the main house, the legend of Mirador's original owners lives on. There are those who say that the ghost of Colonel Bowen's wife haunts the room in which she died. Reputedly the old lady appears just in time to undress any guest who has come to spend the night!

Typical of the great Virginia manor houses that are

LEFT: *Hand-painted Chinese wall coverings, a herringbone parquet floor and Chippendale mouldings embellish the music room.* BELOW: *A grand setting where countless friends and luminaries have been entertained over the years by the various owners, the dining room includes elaborate paneling, a corbeled cornice with egg and dart design, a marble mantel by the Brothers Adam, and French doors to a terrace.* BOTTOM: *In the small drawing room, friends can gather around a fireplace which has a carved Adam mantel.*

legion against the panorama of the Blue Ridge are a host of estate and farm buildings: a fine stable suitable for polo ponies, pleasure horses or prized Thoroughbreds; six tenant houses including the handsome "Chiswell," nestled in the woodlands; the swimming pool, tennis court and indoor sports complex; and other attendant structures totalling 16 buildings in all.

From the main barn, with its turkey weather vane atop the cupola, the scene is a classic, with miles of neat white fencing and gravel roads, pastures sloping down to ponds, hills rising to meet the woodlands, and Georgian architecture echoing the quiet dignity of Virginia's past generations.

Photography by Robert Llewellyn.

Mirador was presented in Unique Homes by Daniel R. O'Neill, Charlottesville, VA.

Harrietta Plantation

Charleston County, South Carolina

Surrounded by giant cypress trees, live oaks and magnolias, the old plantation house stands near the South Santee River and surveys a landscape rich with color, whether it be the blooms of azaleas, camelias and dogwood, or the rice fields quietly silhouetted in the fading light of sunset. Architecturally, it displays both Federal and Greek Revival influences, while the exterior and interior trim are completely unified in the elegant, restrained style of Adam. The black cypress of which the homestead was built is as sound as when it was first cut and seasoned. Having been "brought up" in the most honorable of Southern traditions, Harrietta is a true aristocrat of plantation homes.

In 1933, the picture of proper plantation life here was depicted in the pages of *The House Beautiful*, in an article written shortly after a modernization of the 17-room residence that has long served as the centerpiece for this sprawling property in McClellanville. Then, visitors were cautioned: "The carriage drive still is used as the driveway, and if one must arrive in a motor, it should be kept as quiet as possible so as not to disturb the deer and birds that claim the place as their heritage." Today as ever, the Lowcountry bows reverently to the land, its lifeblood continuing to course through rich tidal marshes, rice beds along the river, salt streams and storm tides.

OPPOSITE TOP: *Located in the "English basement" is the breakfast room, originally the gun room. This cozy space is characterized by arched windows, elegant mouldings and a fireplace.* OPPOSITE BOTTOM: *The plantation house was built in 1795 by Mrs. Harriott Pinckney Horry of neighboring Hampton Plantation for her daughter, Harriott, as a wedding present. Today the home is listed on the National Register of Historic Places.* ABOVE: *The classic beauty of the manor's facade is accented by white pillared porticoes, wrought iron balustraded balconies and exquisitely pedimented eaves. Shown here is the north portico entrance.*

Property size: Approximately 1,016 acres in four natural tracts.

Architectural style: Southern Colonial plantation manor, with Federal and Greek Revival influences, on the National Register of Historic Places.

When built: Started in 1795. Modernized in the 1930s; extensive restoration from 1981 to 1984.

Number of rooms: 17.

Square footage: 7,947±.

Number of bedrooms: Four to six.

Number of baths: Four full, three half-baths.

Outbuildings: Five guest cottages, boat house, manager's house, two stable buildings plus various farm structures.

Distinctive features: Exterior of English brick, pine and black cypress; white pillared porticos. Interior includes heart pine floors, pocket doors, superb mantelpieces, high ceilings and crystal chandeliers. "English basement" with breakfast room and full kitchen; wine, vegetable and preserves cellars. Contemporary conveniences include central air conditioning and modern baths.

Additional highlights: A well-documented plantation house situated within a sporting plantation on the South Santee River, 45 miles north of Charleston. Extensive gardens featured on the grounds immediately surrounding the residence. Property includes 173 acres of diked and managed duck marshes and fish ponds, equestrian facilities and fields abundant with wildlife.

The approach to Harrietta Plantation is all Southern grace and symmetry. An avenue canopied in live oaks leads to wrought iron balconies and white pillared porticos encircling the home, commissioned in 1797 by Mrs. Harriott Pinckney Horry as a wedding gift for her daughter, also named Harriott. Of the ensuing years, historian Samuel Gaillard Storey has written, "The home was never lived in until 1858 because as each heir came of age, some unforeseen circumstances prevented his making it his home." Many attribute the design of the residence to Thomas Pinckney, an architect of Thomas Jefferson's day and, ironically, a vice presidential candidate on the same ticket with Jefferson.

Though empty for its first 60 years, the home was well cared for and never subject to decay or vandalism. And, in large part due to modern necessities added in the 1930s, along with an extensive three-year restoration in the 1980s, Harrietta Plantation remains every bit the belle of antebellum life.

OPPOSITE TOP: *Hauntingly beautiful is the spectacle of the moon shining over rice fields which have been inundated by the river at high tide.* OPPOSITE BOTTOM: *Intricate mouldings, ceilings over 12 feet in height, pocket doors and rich heart pine floors are among the appointments gracing the main rooms of the manor house.* BELOW: *From the east portico, views of rice fields and the South Santee River unfold. The plantation has almost one mile of river frontage in addition to over a mile of frontage along Collins Creek, which includes a dock for river access.*

A fire glows in the breakfast room of the "English basement," a sporty, brick-floored lounge where the men gather before heading out for a morning of duck shooting. Upstairs the reception rooms are filled with 12-foot ceilings, heart pine floors, crystal chandeliers and fine mantelpieces—all original to the manor house. A Palladian doorway opens into the long hall from which the main rooms branch, while wings and porches extend the layout east and west. Despite its size of nearly 8,000 square feet, the home is never more than one room deep, part of the architect's original plan to maximize both views and cross-ventilation.

There have been few cosmetic changes to the original residence built of brick, cypress and pine, though today Harrietta does offer modern baths, central air conditioning and other conveniences such as the stereo and bar housed in a passageway between the drawing room and library.

ABOVE: *A beautifully carved mantel is the focal point of the English-style library. Throughout the residence, remarkably detailed original mantels embellish many of the rooms.* OPPOSITE TOP: *One of five attractive guest houses located on the property.* OPPOSITE BOTTOM: *French wallpaper hand-painted in China adds a colorful complement to the classic woodwork, open staircase and heart pine flooring in the entry hall.*

While much has been written about the decoration and detail of this National Register home, it remains inescapably dwarfed by the scope of the plantation as a whole. Surrounding the mansion is the plantation's principal tract (336 of the approximately 1,016 acres), which abounds with deer, dove and wild turkey and includes 173 acres devoted to diked and managed duck marshes and fish ponds. Close to home, walls and walkways of old English brick lead to the gardens and guest cottages. Further removed, the manager's cottage and stable buildings oversee silos, pastures and paddocks.

And beyond all of this, the South Santee River delta and hundreds of thousands of acres of "forever wild" lands—including a coastal reserve and national wildlife refuge—surround Harrietta Plantation in the lazy, moss-draped beauty of the Lowcountry.

Photography by N. Jane Iseley.

Harrietta Plantation was presented in Unique Homes by Alson Goode, McClellanville, SC.

Whitehall

The Former Home of Golfing Great Bobby Jones

—— *Atlanta, Georgia* ——

The year was 1929. The city was Atlanta. And two men were on their way to becoming legends. One was Bobby Jones, a strapping 20-year-old described by biographer Charles Price as "purely and simply a genius at golf." By the tender age of 28, Jones had 13 titles under his belt and had won 62% of all the national championships he entered in Great Britain and the United States. Four of these titles were won within a single season, earning Jones the Grand Slam. Price continues, "No amateur or professional golfer before or since has come close to compiling such a record, and nobody with any sense could imagine that anybody else ever will."

The second up-and-coming legend was Georgia native Philip Trammell Shutze, born in Columbus in 1890 and a member of the first graduating class of architecture at Georgia Tech. One year later he received an additional degree from Columbia University, and by 1915 he had been awarded the Prix de Rome, affording him a program of study at the American Academy in Rome. For Shutze, this was just the start of a life-long love affair with classi-

ABOVE: *The rear facade opens to a brick terrace, from which steps descend to the large pool area.* OPPOSITE TOP: *Inspired by a Northern Italian villa in Serlio, architect Philip Trammell Shutze designed Whitehall in 1929, and later oversaw the changes to the layout made by Bobby Jones.* OPPOSITE BOTTOM: *Jones built the rustic lodge seen here as a casual retreat for entertaining guests. It includes an oversized stone fireplace, an all-wood gymnasium and a cedar deck.*

cism, a style he brought to Atlanta in 1929.

The estate Shutze created in Buckhead that year was patterned after one of his favorite residences—a Northern Italian villa in Serlio. For his clients, Dr. and Mrs. Leroy Childs, he utilized all the classical motifs along with fabulous mouldings, niches, plasterwork, wood carvings and marble balustrades, while combining many modern comforts and practical details. A decade after the home's completion, and four years after his professional "retirement" in 1935, Bobby Jones was united with the house that seemed destined to become his greatest trophy. He called upon Shutze to help him make custom changes to his new home, Whitehall.

The second-floor sleeping porch was enclosed with Palladian windows in its conversion to Mr. Jones' study. An elevator was installed to rise from the living room to the master suite. A rustic log cabin lodge was built on the tree-bowered grounds out back, providing a wonderful pavilion for casual gatherings complete with gymna-

CHARACTERISTICS

Property size: 8.6 acres in Buckhead.

Architectural style: Neo-classical Italianate villa.

When built: 1928-1929; expanded in 1939; continuously upgraded since 1971.

Outbuildings: New three-car garage with upstairs suite; beautiful log cabin with gymnasium and cedar deck.

Distinctive features: Slate roof, European stone balustrades, Corinthian columns, marble floors, wide French doors, elevator, terraces, upper-level wrought iron balcony. Superb original mouldings, niches, window framing, plasterwork and wood carvings; abundant use of marble throughout. Established grounds of magnolias, oaks, dogwoods and fruit trees; on-site putting and chipping greens, 70-foot swimming pool, badminton court, terra cotta patios.

Additional highlights: Located on Tuxedo Road in the prestigious Buckhead area of Atlanta, Whitehall was conceived by eminent architect Philip Trammell Shutze, a native of Georgia who received much of his early training in Italy. A Northern Italian villa in Serlio was the inspiration for this home, which remains filled with many classical elements, among them gilded columns, marble floors and Palladian windows. It was the site of the 1991 Atlanta Decorator's Showhouse; also a showhouse in 1978.

sium and badminton court. On the cedar deck, the golfing great would enjoy cocktails and conversation with friends including Coca-Cola magnate Robert Woodruff, industrialist Cliff Roberts, Atlanta newspaper baron Clark Howell, Jr., and banker Robert Maddox. Here, too, it is remembered that Jones and his coterie sparked the Ike-for-President campaign of 1952.

Bobby and Mary Jones, along with children Clara, Bobby and Mary Ellen, lived at Whitehall until 1971. It was very much a private place, a home of intimacy and enchantment amid more than eight acres of gardens and lawns, a profusion of magnolias and oaks, dogwoods and fruit trees, and of course custom-tailored greens for chipping and putting. In 1978, Atlanta had its first inside look at Whitehall when it was selected as the year's Decorator's Showhouse, an honor which was once again bestowed in 1991.

The original facade was of wood covered in a paint mixed with sand to resemble limestone. Today, it is a soft vanilla-colored stucco embraced by elegant gardens and sweeping terraces. The commanding entrance, with its original black and white marble floor, leads to a sun-drenched living room and a library adorned with gilded columns, richly glazed walls and a marble-faced fireplace. The terrace room contained Mr. Jones' countless trophies. The dining room was a showcase for his porcelain

OPPOSITE TOP & ABOVE: A mood of formal elegance characterizes the living room, featuring a handsome fireplace, elaborate woodwork and exquisite crystal chandelier. Design by John Craft Interiors. OPPOSITE BOTTOM: The original black and white marble floor and a staircase that sweeps around a chandelier highlight the entrance foyer. Design by Sanford Thigpen Interiors. LEFT: Views of the pool area and rear grounds unfold through the oversized windows in the breakfast room. Design by Carol Klotz Interiors.

collection. The area once used for upstairs staff quarters now houses a spacious family room, and the Bobby Jones study on this floor has been transformed into a gold and marble spa bath that is unabashedly bacchanalian. A 70-foot swimming pool is the most recent addition.

Bobby Jones was a golfing legend with a personality that could "charm the blossoms off a peach tree," but few knew this modest fellow was also an avid student of engineering, English literature and law (he passed the Georgia state bar exam when only half-way through his second year at Emory). His interests were as far-reaching as his drives; his insight was as on target as his putts that would "die" in the hole. It seems fitting that Jones made Whitehall his home, for it is the work of an architect whose talents were equally remarkable.

Photography by David Schilling, Schilling Photography, Atlanta, GA.

Whitehall was presented in Unique Homes by Susan Perkins, Coldwell Banker/Previews®, Atlanta, GA.

OPPOSITE TOP: *An old world elegance pervades the library. Design by C. Smith Grubbs Interiors.* OPPOSITE BOTTOM: *Palladian-style windows accentuate the sun room. Design by Kathy Guyton Interiors.* TOP: *The beautifully updated kitchen is ready to handle all the demands of family living and grand entertaining.* LEFT: *The home's unerring attention to detail is even evident in the guest bathroom. Design by Haynes Robinson.* ABOVE: *The formal dining room. Design by James Essary & Associates.*

Reinterpreting the Prairie Style

Isleworth, Windermere, Florida

"We looked at this as an opportunity to create a home that paid faithful homage to Frank Lloyd Wright's Prairie style, while at the same time provided every contemporary comfort," says Joan Des Combes of her recently completed residence in the posh lakeside Isleworth enclave of Windermere/Orlando. And what she and husband Roland ultimately accomplished was a home of which they never cease to be in awe. "The detailing is so extensive," says Joan, "sometimes I forget a certain fitting or treatment and I marvel at it all over again, as if seeing it for the first time."

Transplanted New Yorkers who head Architectural Artworks Inc., an architectural and interior design firm in central Florida, the Des Combes wanted to create a liveable work of

OPPOSITE: *The double-story grand salon features a spectacular lake view, an elaborately detailed cherry library and media center, and a massive curved granite fireplace.* ABOVE: *Nestled among mature oaks, this lakefront home pays homage to Frank Lloyd Wright's Prairie-style architecture with its shallow hipped roofs, wide roof overhangs and single-story wings branching out from the main two-story structure. The setting is Isleworth, Arnold Palmer's premier golf and country club community in the Windermere area of Orlando.*

CHARACTERISTICS

Property size: Three-quarters of an acre (lakeside).
Architectural style: Modeled after Frank Lloyd Wright's Prairie style.
When built: 1991.
Number of rooms: 12.
Square footage: 6,000.
Number of bedrooms: Four.
Number of baths: Four and one-half.
Outbuildings: Studio or guest quarters.
Distinctive features: Beautifully fitted and detailed mouldings, flooring and cabinetry. Flooring materials include flamed granite, cherry parquet and walnut with ash inlay. All fabrics, wall coverings, light fixtures, mouldings and windows faithfully replicated in the Wright style.
Special distinctions: Winner of two 1992 Aurora Awards, one for "Overall Custom Home," and the second for "Custom Kitchen."
Additional highlights: Lovely lakefront setting in Isleworth, a private country club development bordering 11 miles of freshwater lakes along the Butler Chain of Lakes. Amenities here include an 18-hole championship golf course by Arnold Palmer, a 63,000-square-foot clubhouse, a tennis center with Har-Tru courts, and 24-hour security.

LEFT: *Noteworthy elements of the staircase include stacked windows, intricate balusters, elaborate newel post and Tiffany-patterned carpet.* BELOW: *The master bedroom, master bath and sitting room overlook the lake through mature oaks. Wall coverings and fabrics are documented Wright designs.*

art, far from the mainstream of typical Florida architecture. They decided on the Prairie style as it so clearly lended itself to the detailing they are noted for: custom-designed staircases, perfectly fitted mouldings and paneling in rare woods, and furnishings that are in keeping with the style.

In their own home, they have filled the rooms with Wright's original barrel chairs and pieces by Le Corbusier. The dining room is all Mackintosh, and the windows are from the Prairie Style series recently introduced by Pella. The 20th century Arts and Crafts movement is very much at home here.

Shallow-hipped roofs, single-story wings emanating from a two-story core, and a natural vista of the lake and live oaks from every room are all true to Wright's organic

ABOVE: *In the grand salon, a rolling ladder provides easy access to the highest shelves.* LEFT: *In addition to the raised paneling and elongated windows shown here, a floor-to-ceiling fireplace and granite hearth grace this room, used by the current owners as an art gallery. The windows frame a view that includes oak trees and lake beyond.*

tradition, and to his credo that "houses should no longer be boxes placed arbitrarily in the landscape." In fact, not one of the 18 live oaks on the lushly canopied grounds was displaced for the construction.

Indoors, a central double-height salon appointed in lustrous cherry wood and with a curving granite fireplace is a focal point for entertaining. Though it's safe to assume guests seldom leave without lingering in the award-winning kitchen, where the cabinetry is built of exotic African mahogany and countertops are surfaced in granite. The more quiet and private areas of the home include four bedrooms, a separate studio building where the Des Combes meet their clients, and a gallery which was planned as an exhibition space—all black and white and sleek—for Roland's unique graphite renderings. He has chronicled many rooms of the Mark Twain House in Hartford as well as some of the grand old summer cottages in the Hamptons.

OPPOSITE: *The dining room features amethyst and cobalt blue Italian Murano lighting fixtures and a walnut and ash inlaid floor.* RIGHT: *Large windows surround the breakfast room with wonderful views.* BELOW: *"African Mahogany" SieMatic cabinetry from Germany, granite countertops, polished porcelain flooring and gourmet appliances make the kitchen luxuriously efficient.*

It is these beautiful drawings, all in perfect scale and perspective, that have become a trademark of their firm. "These are not your typical floor plans with an overhead view," explains Joan, "but actual drawings of what each room will look like when you're standing in it. At first glance, they look like photographs." Considering their experience in construction management, architecture and design, the Des Combes are a rare find in Orlando. And, as Joan suggests, they are fluent in the ability to tailor each project to an environment truly wedded to the lifestyle and tastes of its owners.

Photography by Everett & Soulé.

This Frank Lloyd Wright-inspired masterpiece was presented in Unique Homes by Isleworth Realty, Inc., Windermere, FL.

Watercolors on Lake Boca

Boca Raton, Florida

The view out over the lake is classic Boca. One stretch along the opposite shore rises all pale pink stucco and red tile rooftops. It's Addison Mizner's original Cloister Inn—now the centerpiece of the Boca Raton Hotel and Club. Beyond, a sweep of emerald defines the fairways Gerald Ford and Frank Sinatra have considered among their favorites. Back at home, coquina stone walls, fountains and flowers fill the approach to this Mediterranean estate. Every turn offers a lush look at the good life Mizner had in mind when he mapped out his master plan for Boca Raton nearly 70 years ago.

Inspired by the majestic Mediterranean villas Mizner first popularized in Palm Beach, this home is a waterfront landmark. Its property is the largest on the lake; its gated setting the most private. Indoors, glass and black granite expose the rooms to a kaleidoscope of light and reflection. Outside, the 6,000-square-foot motor court of interlocking pavers is offset on the opposite side by another 4,000 square feet devoted to outdoor entertaining. The

OPPOSITE TOP: *The view across Lake Boca Raton at sunset.* OPPOSITE BOTTOM: *Complete with sitting area and elegant his-and-her baths, the first-floor master suite also opens out to a water-view patio.* RIGHT: *Boasting 150 feet of water frontage, this is the largest property on the lake. Included are premier docking facilities, a heated pool and large outdoor entertaining area.* BELOW: *A billiards area adjoins the second-floor family room.* BOTTOM: *Local artist Raymond Karpuska designed the custom sit-down bar, featuring detailed sides of stainless steel and a granite top.*

CHARACTERISTICS

Property size: Two and one-half lots (just under an acre) fronting Lake Boca Raton.
Architectural style: Mizner-style Mediterranean.
Square footage: 10,000±.
Number of bedrooms: Five (all suites).
Number of baths: Six full, two half-baths.
Distinctive features: Granite floors, an abundance of glass, Poggenpohl kitchen cabinetry, main-level master suite with two baths, elevator, media room, heated diving pool with glass block waterfall and spa, 4,000-square-foot outdoor entertainment center overlooking the water. Porte cochere entrance with coquina stone walls, fountains and over $200,000 in landscaping.
Additional highlights: This is the largest residential property on Lake Boca Raton, and it is considered the city's finest waterfront setting. A private finger pier offers dockage space for 80-foot and 60-foot yachts, plus a 15,000-pound hydraulic lift accommodating a 48-foot yacht.

diving pool and spa, copper-roofed gazebo and bar, terraces and yacht-size pier all afford stellar views.

Perhaps the only thing missing is Mizner himself, who no doubt would be somewhat amused by the domestic luxuries that have appeared since his day, among them: 10 zones of central air conditioning, Poggenpohl kitchen cabinetry and every gourmet appliance, a media room reached by elevator, the 15,000-pound vertical hydraulic lift at dockside, and computerized security indoors and out.

Photography by Luxury Florida Homes.

This estate was presented in Unique Homes by Corinne Brinkman and Dorothy Snyder, Luxury Homes, Inc., Boca Raton, FL.

Entertaining Ideas

The Sanctuary, Boca Raton, Florida

A masterpiece of contemporary design built a decade ago on a southeast point in the Sanctuary, this home has served its owners well. Family entertaining is a regular occurrence here, and the variety of activities the property affords both indoors and out facilitates gatherings of any size. For the owners, entertaining can be as easy as a barefoot barbecue in a gazebo on the pool terrace; or as elaborate as a formal dinner for 12 beneath a crystal chandelier, and perhaps a movie afterwards in the theatre/media room, acoustically perfect and plush with deep-seated sofas and chaises. After the guests are gone, the hosts retreat to their own quarters where the walls are padded in silk, a Jacuzzi awaits in the bath, and the

CHARACTERISTICS

Property size: Oversized corner lot with 180 feet of deep-water frontage.
Architectural style: Florida contemporary.
When built: 1983.
Number of rooms: 12.
Square footage: 11,000.
Number of bedrooms: Five or six.
Number of baths: $10^1/_2$.
Distinctive features: Soaring three-story layout with water views from every sight line. Sweeping cantilevered, curved staircase of imported glass, custom millwork, floor-to-ceiling fireplace of Philippine fossil stone, open bridge on the second floor connecting north and south wings, first-floor maid's quarters or guest suite, media and game rooms.
Special amenities: Third-floor exercise salon, large elevator, two of every major appliance in kitchen, computerized home management system.
Additional highlights: Ultimate design for living/entertaining on the water in the Sanctuary. Included are 170-foot docking facilities with no fixed bridges to the ocean, a free-form pool with special-effect lighting and waterfall/spa, poolside cabana and gazebo with wet bar and barbecue.

windows open to a soothing overview of water.

The home, known as Sanctuary Point, has been planned with the best of Boca in mind, from the 170-foot deep-water dock to the million dollars or so the owners have invested in custom accoutrements. There's a computerized home management system accessed in both the kitchen and master suite. There's a top-floor gym complete with mirrored work-out area, treadmill, exercise bike, massage table and built-in TV and stereo. There's an elevator to whisk you from the wine room to the Jacuzzi in the master suite in a jiffy. And throughout, water in all its forms—splashing into the pool, lapping at dockside, cascading from a tiered fountain at the entry—provides a perfect focus. The endless surfaces of mirror

and glass add further dimension to the design of the 11,000-square-foot interior.

Buffered by the beauty on a 27-acre natural preserve and the quiet cachet of the Sanctuary, the home has instant access to the enclave's own tennis and marina facilities and is close to all in-town activities. Many who have visited, though, say the main attraction is right at home, and there's really no reason to look beyond.

Photography by Brian Aker.

This waterfront home in the Sanctuary was presented in Unique Homes by Dorothy Snyder and Corinne Brinkman, Luxury Homes, Inc., Boca Raton, FL.

OPPOSITE TOP: *The home oversees 180 feet of water frontage.* OPPOSITE BOTTOM: *The game room comes with a custom pool table and a full-service bar.* TOP: *Window walls overlook the heated free-form pool and waterway beyond.* ABOVE LEFT: *The formal guest suite.* ABOVE RIGHT: *The two-level theatre-style media room.*

Casa Apava

Palm Beach, Florida

ABOVE: *From Casa Apava's oceanfront stone terrace, a large expanse of lawn sweeps down to the beach.* RIGHT: *Set amid a sea of royal palms, Casa Apava boasts over 400 feet of ocean frontage as well as wonderful views of Lake Worth. It is undoubtedly one of the finest estate properties ever built in Palm Beach.*

In the rip-roaring twenties, or as one Palm Beach hostess used to say, "Back when my 'old money' was simply called 'money'," architect Abram Garfield, son of the 20th President of the United States, and developer Paris Singer collaborated on a home that was virtually unrivaled for Palm Beach. It was a Moorish and Mediterranean palace, perhaps surpassed in grandeur by Marjorie Merriweather Post's 120-room Mar-a-Lago, but nonetheless an oceanfront gem, from its sun-swept beach to the tower rising above the royal palms. Beneath barrel tile rooftops, it remains one of the *grandes dames* of Palm Beach, with the ocean to the east, the lake to the west, and a fantasy of pink-beige stucco, velvety lawns and tropical gardens in between.

Casa Apava (apava coming from Sanskrit literature, meaning "he who sports in the water") bespeaks a classic Spanish style in the array of earth tones and colored tiles, the myriad nooks, alcoves and balconies, its stone fireplaces, cascading fountains, and French windows and doors at every turn. Off a terrace surrounding the 60-foot saltwater pool is the romantic library, complete with minstrel gallery and a vaulted, hand-stenciled ceiling. On the third floor, a small spiral staircase winds its way up to the belvedere tower room, an open aerie overlooking the sea. Amid the pool views and exquisite paneling, one can well imagine the moonlit galas of days gone by.

From the castellated entry to the dining room, floored in a sea of meridian-blue tile, all the irreplaceable old world touches remain. The formal sitting room has an open cast stone fireplace and beamed and stenciled ceiling. A second-floor writing nook leads on to an intimate terrace overlooking the lake. The master suite has French doors which open to reveal a view that stretches out to sunrises over the ocean.

Casa Apava also responds in all the right ways to the modern world. In addition to the main kitchen, which is well equipped for grand-scale entertaining, there's a brand-new service kitchen with European cabinets, wine cooler and first-rate appliances. Two private apartments are available for staff. Offices are conveniently placed on the first and second floors of the main house. Six of the seven principal bedrooms have fireplaces, and all have luxurious, modern baths. A Har-tru tennis court is included on the beautifully landscaped grounds. Among the most recent improvements made to the estate are eight zones of all-new heating and air conditioning, upgraded phone and cable lines, new electrical service throughout the majority of the house, a landscape irrigation system, and new terraces and fountains surrounding the re-tiled pool.

For some 70 years, this landmark has been the much-admired centerpiece of the estate section of town, along South Ocean Boulevard just south of the Bath & Tennis Club. Its 420 feet of oceanfront and more than five acres of lushly planted privacy could scarcely be duplicated today, as is the case with the residence itself—one of the great beauties in a town where luxury and loveliness mean everything.

Casa Apava was presented in Unique Homes by Martha A. Gottfried, Inc., Palm Beach, FL.

LEFT: *French doors framing ocean views, tile flooring and a fireplace create an elegant ambience in the formal dining room.* ABOVE: *The Spanish influence on the home's design can be seen in the stucco exterior topped with a red barrel tile roof. Shown here is the eastern facade.* BELOW: *The formal sitting room is a magnificent entertaining space with its large, open cast stone fireplace, intricate ceiling treatment including stenciled beams, and new flooring of walnut.*

CHARACTERISTICS

Property size: Five and one-quarter-acre oceanfront parcel.

Architectural style: Moorish and Mediterranean mansion.

When built: 1920s. Extensive modernization in 1987.

Square footage: Approximately 15,000.

Number of bedrooms: Seven (not including staff accommodations).

Number of baths: Six full, four powder rooms.

Distinctive features: Quarry keystone entry, red barrel tile roof above facade of stucco, original paneling and vaulted ceilings, refinished floors throughout, exceptional tile work, French doors and windows, terraces, balconies, tower room rising above third floor. All but one of the principal bedrooms have fireplaces, and there are fireplaces as well in the sitting room, dining room, library and morning room.

Special amenities: First-rate security system, commercial-grade kitchen appliances, upgraded plumbing and electrical systems.

Additional highlights: Heated 30' x 60' pool economically fed by salt water. One of Palm Beach's premier estates, Casa Apava combines a wealth of old world details with luxurious modern comforts.

The Riviera Refined

Key Biscayne, Florida

The swimming pool says it all. Even if you dive deep, you don't miss the music. There are hundreds of stereo speakers indoors and out, plus a few underwater as well. And, as the sun sets over Biscayne Bay, you can wrap up your laps with a swim up to the bar. The service area is high and dry, but the seating arrangement is submerged in crystal-clear water. This is the laid-back life deluxe of Key Biscayne, in a home that combines the sizzle of Miami with the romance of the Caribbean.

Completed in 1989 for a private investor native to Honduras, the villa on Harbor Point Drive has one of the most envied settings around. It's just two houses down the road from the former winter White House of Richard Nixon, and one of only two properties on Key Biscayne with open bay waters to one side, and a protected inner channel mooring on the other. The sun rises dockside, bathing the gated entry and east facade in brightness, and it sets over the terraces and pool, lingering

OPPOSITE: *A magnificent villa in the Mediterranean style, this Key Biscayne residence of approximately 13,000 square feet boasts the rarity of open bay frontage on one side and protected safe dockage on the other.* ABOVE: *Complete with underwater speakers, a Jacuzzi and a unique sunken bar, the custom pool area invites outdoor living at its finest—all against a backdrop of breathtaking bay views. Balconies off the rear facade offer additional opportunities for family members and guests to enjoy the spectacular panorama that unfolds over the water.*

against a horizon of bay waters and the skyline in the distance. To the north and south, elaborate gardens, numerous palm trees and verdant lawns sequester the Mediterranean mansion in an oasis of tropical splendor.

A soft palette of pastels tempers the waterfront panorama, from brilliant aqua in the morning to the silvered hues of dusk. Curtaining the double-height living room are window coverings of robin's egg blue, tasselled back to reveal the forever views of Biscayne Bay. In the cabana, wide stripes of celadon and salmon add a festive

LEFT: *The entry courtyard immediately establishes a Mediterranean theme for the property. Located above the three-car garage are separate quarters.* OPPOSITE BOTTOM: *The home includes its own fully equipped gym as well as an indoor racquetball court.* BELOW: *The gourmet kitchen is centered around a granite-topped island and adjoins a breakfast area with etched glass accents and built-ins.* BOTTOM: *Rising two stories and crowned by a lavish chandelier, the living room is a stunning entertaining space with its exquisite mouldings, soaring wall of windows framing water views, and two sets of French doors opening to keystone terraces overlooking the pool.* BOTTOM LEFT: *The master suite's private outdoor Jacuzzi captures a wonderful bay view.*

touch to the tented ceiling. The master bedroom is draped and canopied in restful tones of melon. Throughout, uninterrupted surfaces of white and rose marble and etched glass provide an elegant and never-overbearing backdrop for important paintings, antiques and family treasures.

While this is a home planned with elaborate opportunities for entertaining, it's also a haven for fun and relaxation. The master suite has its own outdoor Jacuzzi, open to the balmy air but privately tucked away from

view. A tasting table serves as the centerpiece for a wine cellar stocked with foreign and domestic labels, including those bearing the owner's name. In the media room on the lower floor, the large saltwater aquarium has been home to a colorful display of shrimp, clownfish and live coral. (For easier maintenance, though, it is presently being converted for freshwater species.) No room or vantage point is without a visual treat, from the

goddess of wine etched into the glass over the custom wet bar, to the brick paved entry where carved lions guard the front gates.

And, it is quite evident that no expense has been spared in providing the home with every last luxury. On sultry nights, one can push a button and instantly air condition the outdoor dining terrace. The grand piano in the living room offers the option of live or computer-

LEFT: *The covered keystone dining terrace is a truly unique outdoor space in that it can be air conditioned.* BELOW: *Located on the main level, the informal living room is a perfect spot from which to enjoy the sunset over Biscayne Bay. This space includes a wet bar, fireplace, built-in entertainment center and terrace access through French doors.* BOTTOM: *Columns and flooring of marble enhance the elegant ambience in the formal dining room.*

programmed playing. In a large storage space on the grounds, an abundant supply of keystone is reserved for any future repairs or improvements. Available only in very limited supplies today, the beautiful coral stone excavated from the ocean floor is used extensively throughout the villa, as are polished granite and lustrous Italian marbles.

For an owner who divides her time between Key

♏ CHARACTERISTICS

Property size: Double-size lot, with back of the house on the open, wide waters of Biscayne Bay; protected water frontage to the front of the property.

When built: 1989.

Square footage: 13,000+.

Number of bedrooms: Four (not including guest or staff quarters).

Outbuildings: Three-car garage with separate quarters above.

Distinctive features: Extensive use of keystone marble tile, etched mirrors, French doors and custom mouldings; wonderful waterfront terraces and private balconies; double-height foyer with floating circular staircase; gleaming white and rose marble floors; wine cellar/pub; custom wet bar with wall of etched glass.

Special amenities: Elevator, extensive stereo speakers throughout property, Jacuzzi on private terrace outside master suite, built-in entertainment center in media/family room, indoor racquetball court, fully equipped gym, state-of-the-art electronics.

Additional highlights: A dramatic gated entrance flanked by statues of lions leads to this palatial Harbor Point property. It is one of only two properties in Key Biscayne that has frontage on the open bay and protected dockage as well.

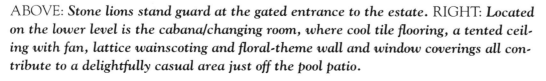

ABOVE: *Stone lions stand guard at the gated entrance to the estate.* RIGHT: *Located on the lower level is the cabana/changing room, where cool tile flooring, a tented ceiling with fan, lattice wainscoting and floral-theme wall and window coverings all contribute to a delightfully casual area just off the pool patio.*

Biscayne and Grand Cayman, it seems only right that her style be a well-orchestrated mix of mainland opulence and island charm, and not without a bit of feminine flair. The 13,000-square-foot villa is anything but a piece of whimsy on the water; it bears a lavish and lasting presence, evoking the palatial Mediterranean villas

of the Riviera. Stone balustrades and wide balconies are balanced beneath orange tile rooftops. From three levels, terraces and French doors open to a view that is one of the world's greatest waterscapes. It is a style that transcends a place or period, and it is a scene of enduring grandeur.

Photography by Florida Showcase Property Directory, Pompano Beach, FL.

This Mediterranean masterpiece was presented in Unique Homes by Evelyn and Meri Framer, Framer Realty, Inc., Miami Beach, FL.

The Brach Estate

— St. Petersburg, Florida —

ABOVE: *The rear facade of the mansion overlooks a sparkling pool and spa.* OPPOSITE TOP: *The focal point of the 85-foot-long foyer is the grand double staircase crafted of mahogany.* OPPOSITE BOTTOM: *The exotic grounds to the rear of the estate feature pathways which wind their way through towering oaks and sun-warmed lawns to the Intracoastal Waterway. Among the outdoor amenities are the heated pool, the spa with fountain and waterfall, the lighted regulation-size tennis court and the deep-water dock with davit.*

Every year in a host of cities around the country, a coterie of top-name designers descend upon a chosen house, rip apart the existing fittings and fabrics, and do their own thing at a frenetic pace to create a Designers' Showhouse. It's all to benefit a wonderful cause—be it a scholarship program or a new hospital wing—and a paying audience eats up the view for a month or more, noting the latest in faux finishes, braided ficus trees and hand-stenciled floors.

In 1991, the Florida Orchestra Designer Showhouse was quite another story. While the orchestra was desperately seeking a home to call a "showhouse," David and Mimi Morritt were undertaking a complete gutting of the Emil Brach mansion on the banks of the Intracoastal in St. Petersburg. "Originally, when we purchased the home in 1988, we were simply going to redecorate," recalls Mimi. "But the interior with its small windows and narrow corridors was impossibly dark...and it was just so rococo." Hence, they began a

RIGHT: *Formal dining is an understatement in this elegant room with fireplace, oak floor and crystal chandelier suspended from a beamed ceiling.* BELOW: *Originally built in the 1920s, the Brach mansion has been transformed through an extensive renovation into a French Mediterranean showplace.* OPPOSITE TOP: *The family room is a bright and cheery living space with custom-crafted entertainment center, informal dining area and access to the dining terrace.* OPPOSITE BOTTOM: *The master suite—complete with wet bar, refrigerator and ice maker—opens to a balcony with commanding views of the rear grounds and Intracoastal Waterway.*

three-year overhaul on the 1920s relic, finishing just in time to open their doors to a benefit which raised over $100,000 for the Florida Orchestra.

A Parisian with a purpose, Mimi saw the inherent beauty of the home—a wonderful mix of Italian, French and Spanish influences—first built for Emil Brach (of the Brach Candy empire). So, as husband David, a London-born real estate developer, commuted to his time-share project at the posh Morritt Tortuga Club in the Cayman Islands, Mimi set out on a project of her own. Walls came down, windows were widened, the den became the dining room, and the grounds, overgrown with years of neglect, were entirely refashioned by the landscape architect from Busch Gardens.

While the whole process was going on, the Morritts

CHARACTERISTICS

Property size: Two and three-quarter acres on the Intracoastal at Boca Ciega Bay.
Architectural style: Provençal villa.
When built: 1925. Renovated extensively from 1988 to 1991.
Number of rooms: 14 in main house; seven in guest house.
Number of bedrooms: Four.
Number of baths: Five full and three half-baths.
Outbuildings: Three-bedroom, three-bath guest house with living and dining rooms, fireplace, wet bar and large kitchen with breakfast room; poolside cabana with bar and barbecue; three-car garage with main house, separate garage for guest house.
Distinctive features: Spanish, French and Italian influences throughout. Elegant archways, marble floors, leaded and stained glass windows, French doors, woodwork hand-milled on the site, 85-foot foyer, mahogany double staircase, four fireplaces and four wet bars. All bedroom suites in the main house have separate air conditioning zones and stereo systems (the house has a total of eight separate heating/air conditioning zones). The master suite includes a private balcony with Intracoastal view; the master bath has a double mother-of-pearl Jacuzzi, imported from England and set in Norwegian marble.
Additional highlights: Electric entrance gates with cameras, new gas-heated pool and spa, new lighted regulation tennis court, dock with davit, stereo speakers and "moonlighting" set in the trees.

moved into a guest house built expressly for the purpose of overseeing the reconstruction. This second home also came in handy as the family watched some 8,000 people tour the main residence during its Designer Showhouse stint last year.

Prior to purchasing the home, Mimi confides, "All I had seen of Florida were Disney World and the Don Cesar Hotel. I didn't think anyone actually lived here!" She remembers how she once told her husband, then working on several developments in Florida and commuting back to the family in London, "Either you stop working in Florida, or we move there." The first house they looked at was the Brach mansion on Park Street.

"We used to have a vacation home on the island of Mallorca, so the climate and architecture felt very familiar." She continues, "And of course our daughters, now ages 18, 16 and 8, fell in love with the place. My youngest insists that she will be married on the grand staircase." It is indeed a wedding cake of a staircase, all mahogany beneath a massive Austrian crystal chandelier, and fronting a foyer some 85 feet in length.

Virtually everything in the home has been replaced, though the French

doors, mahogany beams and the stained glass in the dining room are original. In addition, much of the antique crown moldings, chair rails, dadoes and lambrequins remain intact. To offset the weight of the 12- to 18-inch-thick brick and block walls, elaborate carvings and archways, the Morritts have washed the home in pastels, cool marbles and lustrous silks. Sunlight prevails, with each room opening to a view of tropical palms, azaleas, century-old oaks and the waterfront. A charming dolphin fountain graces the entrance, and a new swimming pool and tennis court await out back.

With great style and dogged determination, and *without* the assistance of two dozen or more celebrated decorators, the Morritts have given new life to a St. Petersburg landmark. "It's all new," says Mimi, "and it all looks like it's been here forever."

Photography by George Cott.

The Brach Estate was presented in Unique Homes by Joanne King Hiller and Rory R. Hiller, Island Estates Realty, Inc., Clearwater, FL.

RIGHT: *Enjoying prime frontage on Sarasota Bay, this stunning home—walled and gated for privacy—offers a 165-foot dock as well as abundant tropical landscaping.* BELOW: *From the veranda, steps lead down to a large terrace which surrounds the heated pool.* OPPOSITE: *Appointments in the spacious living/dining room include a 17-foot vaulted ceiling, marble flooring and a full wall of windows and glass doors opening to the veranda.*

Magnificence on Sarasota Bay

———— Sarasota, Florida ————

You enter a tropical refuge of Cuban laurel, bamboo, black olive trees and bougainvillea. You gaze upon mangroves and breezy queen palms. You gather on a dock that reaches more than 150 feet into Sarasota Bay. Your perspective on the good life has already improved, and you have not yet stepped foot on the private beach, made a ripple in the pool, or toured the light, lofty contemporary residence that is the centerpiece of this Gulf Coast property.

Water views dominate all the rooms, and the dimensions grow gloriously through 15-foot ceilings, vaulted dormers, walls of glass and upper-level balconies. The main living/dining area—over 800 square feet—begins with a marble-floored foyer and doesn't end until it opens onto a wraparound veranda overlooking the pool, beach and bay. Sharing a similar panorama of blue is a glassy breakfast nook off the kitchen, where floors and counters are surfaced in Portuguese granite.

Property size: Approximately one bayfront acre.
Architectural style: Post-modern Mediterranean.
Number of rooms: Nine.
Square footage: 3,500±.
Number of bedrooms: Three.
Number of baths: Three.
Distinctive features: Walls of windows to maximize bay and city views, cathedral ceilings, two fireplaces, European cabinetry, tiled balconies, floors of marble and Portuguese granite.
Special amenities: 165-foot private dock, deeded beach access, custom stereo system, electric dumbwaiter, heated pool and spa.
Additional highlights: Surrounding mangroves provide a natural privacy barrier. Wraparound veranda offers a superb entertaining area overlooking the water.

The master suite is a fitting compliment to its owners; it is a retreat well planned for every last luxury. In a wing all its own are the master bedroom and sitting room, each with fireplace and French doors opening to a balcony and the balmy bayfront, plus a dressing area, walk-in closet and skylighted bath with whirlpool tub. No less elaborate in design are the two additional bedrooms for family members or guests.

Walled, gated and thick with plantings throughout its one-acre setting, the home is, above all, one of the most private properties to be found on the Lido-St. Armands bayfront. Long after the sun has set on Florida's west coast, when the pool is still and reflective, when the palm fronds dance in the wind and the night lights bring on a new sense of drama, it is difficult to imagine being anyplace else.

Photography by Dick Dickinson.

This property was presented in Unique Homes by Michael Saunders & Company, Sarasota, FL.

The Verandah

— The Oaks, Sarasota, Florida —

The Florida room and screened lanais are well positioned to bring in the bright blue of the bay. The dock outside offers an easy invitation to a day of deep-sea fishing in the Gulf of Mexico. Mirrored in the reflecting pool are breezy palms and the blazing sunsets for which Sarasota is famous. Indoors, the view is pronounced with walls of glass and steeply pitched cathedral ceilings. This is the home known as "The Verandah."

Artist Don Freedman's design for this waterfront residence in The Oaks borrows on both the at-the-beach romance of the Caribbean and the sophistication of an elite, gate-guarded address. Pavilions flanking the porte cochere are casual and breezy. Formal areas are polished and flowing. To one side, it's all tropical lushness; to the other, it's an open canvas of water and sky. Sandy tones are used extensively in the decor, with a natural complement of sunshine and refreshing Gulf Coast air adding to the openness of the approximately 8,000-square-foot residence.

The home best succeeds in its plan to provide a setting to match any mood. A friendly dinner by the fire awaits in a country dining room that is open to the magnificent kitchen. Beneath the vaulted, bleached wood ceiling of the huge living room, a sweep of marble and glass presents a shimmering backdrop for cocktails against the purples and pinks of the setting sun. A full-length verandah overlooking the pool adds a luxuriant dimension to the bedroom suites on the upper floor. And regardless of the occasion, the bay-side terrace takes its cue from the water, providing a sun-drenched spot for private sunning and swimming, and an intimate destination for an evening under the stars.

Photography by Dick Dickinson.

The Verandah was presented in Unique Homes by Kathleen Meador, Michael Saunders & Co., Sarasota, FL.

LEFT: *A vaulted cathedral ceiling of bleached wood, cool marble flooring, and bay views lend an inviting Caribbean flair to the 800-square-foot living room. With easy access to the screened bay-view lanais, this room is a natural for entertaining on any scale.*
ABOVE: *Night lighting accentuates the exotic charm of the home.* OPPOSITE: *Looking at the rear facade from the bayfront terrace, it is easy to see why this delightful residence is called "The Verandah."*

CHARACTERISTICS

Architectural style: Caribbean-inspired contemporary.

Square footage: 8,000+.

Number of bedrooms: Five (not including staff accommodations).

Number of baths: Six.

Distinctive features: Vaulted cathedral ceilings, vast expanses of glass to maximize bay views, screened lanais, 800-square-foot living room with huge wood-burning fireplace, raised fireplace in kitchen/dining area, porte cochere.

Additional highlights: Boat dock with davits, separate staff quarters with private entrance, lush landscaping, easy access to fabulous boating and fishing in the Gulf of Mexico.

The Showcase
of Lighthouse Point

Longboat Key, Florida

Lighthouse Point—a private development of waterfront estates occupying a 13-acre peninsula at the southernmost tip of Longboat Key—is hardly your typical Florida luxury community. With a total of only 16 residences sequestered behind a gated entry and surrounded by the waters of New Pass Channel, Sarasota Bay and the Gulf of Mexico, this exclusive enclave offers residents a 25-meter pool, tennis court, landscaped pavilion and private boat docks, plus all the amenities of one of Florida's finest resorts, the Longboat Key Club. When the Colorado architectural firm of Knudson & Gloss was called upon to create a showplace residence within the confines of Lighthouse Point, they rose to the occasion with a design that exemplifies the best aspects of the Florida lifestyle, yet can in no way be considered "typical."

Inside, the drama of the layout is achieved by combining spacious dimensions with lavish embellishments and state-of-the-art amenities. Thassos Italian marble is used not only to create elegant flooring, but also to distinguish the hearths and surrounds of the see-through fireplace which connects the living and family rooms. In the master bath suite, Rosso Levante European marble accentuates an area that includes an exercise room and a

steam shower with temperature-controlled rain dome and rain bar. Berloni cabinetry imported from Italy can be found in the kitchen and butler's pantry, while the media center in the family room comes complete with a Mitsubishi big-screen TV and an integrated sound system with surround sound as well as an infrared remote-controlled Prologic receiver wired to Bose Acoustimass speakers throughout. Upstairs, a large loft area and bridge overlook the double-height living room, family room and entry.

Outside, the attention to detail is no less impressive, from the lush entry courtyard with tiered fountain, to the exterior walks and decks, all of which feature Adoquin Mexican quarry stone with marble inlays. The striking rear facade of the residence is wonderfully reflected in the swimming pool, shaped to complement the architectural lines of the house. Tying the setting together, the pool's disappearing edge brilliantly melds pool deck, landscaping and superb waterfront view into one spectacular canvas. It is architecture raised to the level of art.

Photography by Peter Turo.

This striking home was presented in Unique Homes by Tangerine Realty Corporation, Longboat Key, FL.

🏛 CHARACTERISTICS

Architectural style: Contemporary.
When built: 1992.
Number of bedrooms: Five.
Number of baths: Five full, two half-baths.
Distinctive features: Thassos marble floors in living and dining rooms, foyer, breakfast room and master bath suite; two-story ceilings in entry, living room and family room; Heat Mirror 66 insulating glass in windows and sliding glass doors, granite slab counters and Berloni cabinetry in kitchen; two-way fireplace; electrically operated skylights with rain sensor; winding curved stairway with fiber optic lighting inlays and clear acrylic railing flowing throughout upstairs loft area; master bath with exercise area, whirlpool, Kallista Raindome steam shower, and dual vanities; media center with big-screen TV and integrated sound system hooked up to Bose Acoustimass speakers throughout.

Additional highlights: Lush entry courtyard with fountain, attached three-car garage, all exterior walks and decks of imported Adoquin Mexican quarry stone with Thassos marble inlays, swimming pool with indigo marcite, disappearing edge and attached spa.

OPPOSITE LEFT: *The view across the rear grounds to New Pass Channel.* OPPOSITE RIGHT: *Generous proportions and good flow are hallmarks of the dramatic layout. In the foreground are the curving staircase and the underside of the second-floor bridge. The living room can be seen in the background.* ABOVE: *The pool area at night.* LEFT: *The rear grounds framed by walls of glass create a panoramic backdrop for the two-story living room, also with marble floor and see-through fireplace.*

In An Enchanted Garden

——— Tuscaloosa, Alabama ———

They devote their days to the things that matter most to them: hosting seated dinners for 230 to raise money for the American Cancer Society or Heart Association, for instance, and spending time with their four grandchildren on the beaches of Gulf Shores. He keeps busy on a 300-acre farm a few miles from town, raising cattle and tending to a wholesale tree nursery. She fills her hours nurturing gardens of roses and white crepe myrtle terraced among the pergolas and parterres. Their home displays a decided preference for the formal and fancy, but it is warmed by a wide Southern smile and the bright Tuscaloosa sun.

The fabulous gardens of this 24-acre estate neighboring North River Yacht Club serve as inspiration for a flower-filled interior. Above the foyer's checkerboard floor of black and white marble, Zuber watercolors depict birds and blossoms among the trees. Wall coverings from the Brunschwig & Fils collection reiterate the garden theme, and cuttings from the grounds bring color to every room. Outside, wisteria-

covered walkways provide a breezy approach to the summerhouse.

When the owner, a native of southern West Virginia, says "I love to entertain," she lives up to her promise in a house that is well prepared, whatever the occasion. East of the grand foyer is the keeping room, warmly appointed in cherry paneling and beams, seven-inch wideboard floors and a fireplace of limestone and slate. Just beyond is the living room, its Belgian fabrics and Waterford chandeliers taking the mood from manorly to museum-like. English antiques from the 17th and 18th centuries find a fitting backdrop here, as do a host of other period pieces, such as the 1880 marble washstand in the powder room, the 19th century bronze chandelier in the mahogany library, and the antique marble inlay surrounding the grill in the kitchen. Throughout the 14,000-square-foot Tudor home, French doors and wide limestone bays open to the gardens and woodlands beyond.

The preparations for parties given here are eased greatly by every gourmet gadget in

OPPOSITE: *Poised gracefully on 24 acres, this Tudor mansion was built in 1989 and reflects the finest in workmanship and materials throughout.*
ABOVE: *Extending an elegant introduction to guests is the grand entry foyer with checkerboard marble floor, garden-theme wall coverings, antique brass chandelier and majestic staircase.*

ABOVE: *Designed with grand-scale entertaining in mind, the living room sets a formal tone with its two Waterford crystal chandeliers, extensive mouldings and marble-faced fireplace.* RIGHT: *The sun porch is a casual gathering spot for family and friends.* OPPOSITE TOP LEFT: *Fabric-covered walls, elegant dentil ceiling mouldings and a Waterford crystal chandelier embellish the banquet-sized dining room.* OPPOSITE BOTTOM LEFT: *The mahogany-paneled library with slate fireplace opens through French doors to the terrace garden.* OPPOSITE TOP RIGHT: *The gourmet kitchen is equipped with top-of-the-line appliances to easily meet the demands of large-scale entertaining.* OPPOSITE BOTTOM RIGHT: *Adjacent to the pool, the summerhouse affords a picture-perfect view of the terrace gardens.*

CHARACTERISTICS

Property size: 24 acres.
Architectural style: English Tudor.
When built: 1989.
Square footage: Approximately 14,000.
Number of bedrooms: Six.
Number of baths: Five.
Outbuildings: Four-car garage, summerhouse.
Distinctive features: Extensive mouldings and custom millwork, 12-foot ceilings, three limestone bay windows, five fireplaces of slate and marble, fine mahogany paneling, designer wall and window coverings, three magnificent Waterford chandeliers, cedar walk-in closets, fur closet, secured room for all fine china and silver, wine cellar, antique entrance gate.
Special amenities: Yamaha stereo systems indoors and out, air filtration and humidification, security and fire alarm systems, landscape sprinklers.
Additional highlights: Impeccable acreage includes manicured lawns and gardens, with white crepe myrtle surrounding pool. Wisteria-covered pergola-style walkway leads to summerhouse. Property is next to North River Yacht Club.

the kitchen, a serving pantry, laundry service room, wine cellar, two-sided wet bar, extensive systems for air filtration, indoor/outdoor stereo and more. When it's just the family and friends for the afternoon, all is casual in the summerhouse overlooking the pool, or on the sun porch convenient to the kitchen and breakfast room.

Above the second-floor bedrooms and play areas reserved for their visiting children and grandchildren is a private hideaway that was most likely designed as a potential apartment or studio. Today, though, it is known simply as "Margaret's attic," and it is where the owner keeps a treasure trove of old finds and family mementos. "I save everything and it all goes into my attic," she laughs. While the attic has a name, the home does not. "We never got around to naming the place and we really should. It deserves one."

Photography by Chip Cooper.

This Tudor estate was presented in Unique Homes by Marilyn Lee, Hamner Real Estate, Tuscaloosa, AL, and Bob Jamison, Jamison & Associates, Tuscaloosa, AL.

Renovation on a Grand Scale

Dallas, Texas

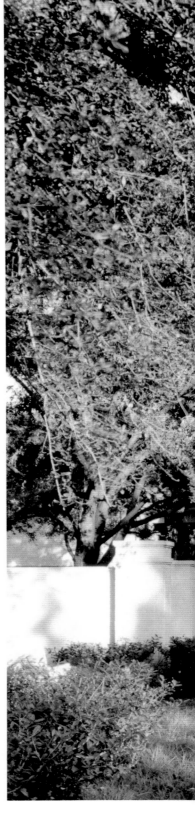

"The hardest part was taking this huge house that was full of cubby holes and all chopped up, undoing a lot of remodeling and literally gutting the home to create warm, liveable space," explains interior designer Barbara Vessels of the house previously owned by the late Algur Meadows, founder of General American Oil. A venerable art collector, Mr. Meadows had purchased the Volk Estates home 11 years after its 1926 construction in what was then the northernmost reaches of Dallas. Built in the English Tudor style, he converted it to part French Normandy, part museum. When the current owners took occupancy in 1982, their first step was to put together a team that could transform an austere relic into a gracious family home.

An article appearing in *Southern Accents* in 1985 explained the assignment: "Reconstruct 70% of the floor plan; replace the heating and cooling systems, wiring and plumbing, and all windows and doors; substantially renovate the exterior, adding a tennis court,

pool, cabana and new garages; provide wall and floor coverings, draperies, furnishings and artwork; and get it done in 12 months, within budget, and with impeccable taste."

Renovations on this scale can often lead to a series of surprises, and this house on Turtle Creek proved no exception. Ms. Vessels explains that when stripping away the horrendous hot pink paint in the living room, they unearthed the original mirrored panels and gold leaf mouldings. These could not be salvaged, but indeed the superb oak herringbone parquetry, original fireplace mantels and chandeliers could.

Perhaps the greatest challenge was the cavernous indoor pool, a huge eyesore rising more than 20 feet and surmounted by what the decorator simply referred to as "one big, ugly square of a skylight." The pool has been filled in and forgotten, and what stands in its place is a series of informal living areas including a family room, bar and guest bedroom with bath. Where there was once a skylight, there is now an antique stained

glass dome Barbara Vessels discovered in New York. The ceiling hardly needed to rise higher, so it was Vessels' idea to bring things down a bit by inverting the dome and suspending it much like a chandelier.

Casual spaces, including the library, card room and billiard room, are intentionally well removed from the formal parlors, reached off a marble-floored foyer and gallery. Custom Taiping carpets and Scalamandré prints soften the space, and Waterford chandeliers shine above. During the year-long renovation, the owner's constant refrain was, "Barbara, are you sure you can warm it up?" What was once a white elephant is now 15,000 square feet of perfect decision-making, from the imported hand-painted Gracie panels in the dining room to the Louis XV desk accompanied by a French Régence chair in the master suite.

When they first saw this house a decade ago, the owners were admittedly apprehensive. In fact, the only thing they were instantly sold on was the estate's pastoral six-acre setting in the heart of one of Dallas' fine

OPPOSITE TOP: *An elegant wood-burning fireplace, classic wall mouldings and matching chandeliers embellish the living room, an enormous and inviting space for grand entertaining.* OPPOSITE BOTTOM: *Beautifully crafted woodwork and built-in shelves frame the marble fireplace and raised marble hearth in the handsome library.* ABOVE: *Originally built in 1926 in the English Tudor style, this beautifully renovated landmark is now reminiscent of a country French manor.*

RIGHT: *From the moment guests enter the marble-floored foyer, they cannot help but be impressed by the wealth of fine appointments and the well-planned flow of the public rooms, all connected by the gracious main gallery shown here.* OPPOSITE: *Oversized windows invite a generous amount of natural light into the formal dining room, where hand-painted Gracie panels create a colorful backdrop for elegant dinner parties.*

old enclaves. They had worked with Barbara Vessels on their previous homes in Dallas and Charlotte, and they knew if this house was going to work for them, so was Barbara. Today, Ms. Vessels returns the compliment with words that would make many a decorator envious: "The easiest part of my job was my clients. They knew what they wanted."

Photography by Peter Paige.

This Dallas landmark was presented in Unique Homes by Kitty T. Snelling, Abio & Adleta, Realtors, Dallas, TX.

CHARACTERISTICS

Property size: Approximately six acres.
Architectural style: Normandy manor, with various elements of its original English Tudor style.
When built: 1926; extensively renovated in 1937, and totally revived in 1982 by present owners.
Number of bedrooms: Five.
Number of baths: Six full, three half-baths.
Outbuildings: Three-car garage, staff cottage, plus poolside pavilion with wet bar and grill.
Distinctive features: All-brick construction with slate mansard roof, high ceilings, deep mouldings, hand-painted Gracie panels, hand-carved fireplaces of wood and marble, large windows, marble-floored foyer, gallery connecting public rooms, card room with wet bar, billiard room, sitting rooms adjoining two of the five bedroom suites. The house is situated on meticulously maintained grounds with tennis court, swimming pool, Jacuzzi and fountain surrounded by wrought iron fencing.
Additional highlights: 70% of the home was reconstructed in the 1980s, with mechanical improvements including all-new plumbing, wiring and six zones of heating and air conditioning. Also, the windows and doors were upgraded. The resulting home is one which accommodates both gracious family living and grand-scale entertaining with ease.

Down Home at the Mayor's Mansion

Houston, Texas

With the infectious laughter and ready smile most Houston ladies seem to be born with, Elise Lanier recently reminisced about the Christmas party of 1989 hosted by her and husband Bob for 800 guests at their River Oaks home. It was barbecue at its biggest (even for Texas), but a bit spicier than usual due to a heated dispute spurred on by then-mayor Kathy Whitmire, who had arrived with fireworks in mind and the press in tow. When the debate over political appointments finally hit the boiling point, Elise realized it was to be an evening no one in Houston would soon forget. The always gracious hostess merely shrugged, "Apparently Mayor Whitmire didn't want to miss a good party!"

These days it's Bob Lanier occupying the mayor's office, and Elise a few doors away overseeing city beautification projects and other good works out of a converted storage room that she rents from the city. Their schedules are full, but when six o'clock comes they're comfortably couched in the study at home with all three televisions going simultaneously. "Once you become a political person you need three TVs," she explains, the "need" word lingering longer than all others.

The study is also their favorite room, where kicking back comes naturally amid family photos and floor-to-ceiling views of the park-like grounds where they've planted more than 2,000 rosebushes. To the front is a grand marble foyer in which the Laniers have greeted guests of honor including Lloyd Bentsen, Ann Richards and Isabella Rossalini. Out back is the 90-foot swimming pool as well as a tennis court where the Israeli tennis team came to play. These two clearly have hosted their fair share of black-tie galas and charity fund-raisers in the 12,000-square-foot Colonial mansion built of century-old bricks from the Waller County Courthouse. But if you ask Elise, it's the country dinners prepared by cook Gloria Jones that keep the guests coming back. The menu seldom varies: fried chicken, yams, cornbread and greens that Lady Bird Johnson says she usually has to wait to return home to get, followed up with home-baked fruit cobbler and a photo opportunity riding a bull in the backyard. Explains Elise, "There's this guy here who rents out these bulls. They just stand there. I think they're all tranquilized!"

OPPOSITE: *Spectacular grounds covering more than two and one-quarter acres include approximately 2,000 rosebushes, formal gardens, a 90-foot pool, a lighted tennis court, and an outdoor dining/sitting area under the spreading 140-year-old oak tree.* LEFT: *Situated on Houston's most prestigious boulevard, this stately Colonial mansion was built in 1971 utilizing century-old bricks from the Waller County Courthouse.*

Their home with its generous mix of elegant and easy spaces seems as giving and versatile as the owners themselves. The formal rooms are exactly that, filled with exquisite mouldings, mantels and other millwork. The casual rooms are numerous, from the third-floor billiard room with its upholstered walls to the morning room, situated off a private walled courtyard planted with seasonal flowers.

"I think what I'll miss most about the house, though, is everything outside," concludes Mrs. Lanier. Here, a few years ago, their staff surprised the mayor and his wife by building a little ranch out back where they could have their barbecues, complete with bales of hay beneath the spreading 140-year-old oak. But the lady of the house is also the lady of city hall, and there's little time for sentimentalizing. It's a hot afternoon in July and the ever-cool Elise interrupts herself on the car phone with one last afterthought. "You know, we just recently had a big dinner here for presidential nominee Bill Clinton. I'd better get working on a party for George Bush." So begins the next big event at the Laniers' River Oaks mansion.

Photography by George Craig.

This River Oaks estate was presented in Unique Homes by Sarah Lee Marks, Howell Properties, Houston, TX.

CHARACTERISTICS

Property size: Approximately two and one-quarter acres in River Oaks.
Architectural style: Plantation-style Colonial mansion.
When built: 1971 (utilizing century-old bricks from the Waller County Courthouse).
Square footage: 12,000±.
Number of bedrooms: Eight.
Number of baths: Six full, several half-baths.
Outbuildings: Carriage house with three-car garage and staff accommodations consisting of a large living/bedroom space, kitchen and full bath; greenhouse; gazebo and mechanical room.
Distinctive features: Classic Colonial style with columned portico leading to grand marble-floored foyer. Second-floor veranda, catering-capacity kitchen with access to morning room, third-floor billiard room/game room with soundproof insulation. Interior is filled with fine mouldings, impressive floating staircase, wide-plank hardwood floors, and distressed cypress paneling. Outdoors are a 90-foot pool with his-and-her dressing rooms, lighted tennis court, alfresco dining area and walled courtyard.
Additional highlights: This is considered one of River Oaks' finest estates. Formal gardens and a monumental oak tree dating back to 1850 enhance the setting, which is convenient to the River Oaks Country Club, Houston's central business district and the Galleria/Post Oak shopping area.

LEFT: *Marble flooring, exquisite mouldings, and an impressive sweeping staircase rising before a wall of glass distinguish the grand entry foyer, which affords a most gracious introduction to the formal and family areas of the first floor.*
ABOVE: *The family room/study—featuring a soaring 24-foot-high beamed ceiling, walls paneled in distressed cypress, expansive windows overlooking the tranquil grounds, and a full-service wet bar—is an ideal space for entertaining friends.*

Derwen Mawr

—— Lake Forest, Illinois ——

The name is translated from the Welsh for "large oak." Before the home was built in 1922, the oaks here were nearly outnumbered by the large families of owls who lived in them. These trees are well remembered in the the fabulous oak pegged floors and beams throughout the home known as Derwen Mawr; the owls, too, continue to have a presence as they are depicted in elaborate carvings on the south facade supporting a bay window in the master suite.

The original owners of this landmark residence on West Deerpath were Mr. and Mrs. Owen Barton Jones, who bought the land, built the original and subsequent portions of the home, and remained here for some 50 years. David Adler, considered one of the most gifted architects of the day, was commissioned to design the east wing in the early 1920s. It was he who laid much of the groundwork for the prevailing Tudor character of the home.

A decade later, Wolcott & Work completed the west wing, its Great Hall entry patterned after an Elizabethan house owned by friends of the Joneses who lived in Berkshire, England. Mr. Jones was so fond of the house known as Sutton Courtney that, after returning to the U.S. from a visit there, he instructed his architect to create a duplicate for Derwen Mawr. So continued the shaping of this authentic English Tudor manor in Lake Forest.

The rooms within the main residence display some of the most remarkable workmanship executed in this country during the 20th century, and the 33 acres of grounds comprise one of the most significant private estates in the area. Drawn by the unlimited potential of this marvelous property, the present owners purchased the home ten years ago and embarked on a significant transformation both indoors and out.

During two years of extensive restoration on the residence and its attendant structures, the owners worked with architect David Easton and his New York office to carefully research and develop the changes necessary to bring the design and decoration of the house to life.

OPPOSITE: *The imposing brick manor house at Derwen Mawr is a Lake Forest landmark. Its east wing was designed by noted architect David Adler in the early 1920s; the west wing was done a decade later by the firm of Wolcott & Work.* LEFT: *Classic details, such as this reflecting pool and handsome brick-walled trellis, abound throughout the estate.* BELOW: *Swans are a common sight on the estate's tranquil pond.*

CHARACTERISTICS

Property size: 33 acres.

Architectural style: Brick and timber Tudor manor.

When built: 1920s. Expanded in the 1930s.
Renovated in 1984-85.

Number of rooms: 20.

Square footage: 11,300±.

Number of bedrooms: Eight (exclusive of staff wing).

Number of baths: Nine.

Outbuildings: Greenhouse, newly renovated two-
story guest house, gatehouse, several garages and
mechanical buildings.

Distinctive features: Oak beams, oak parquet
floors, quarry tile and fossil tile flooring, custom
thermopane mullioned windows, elaborate carvings,
wine-tasting room, and a Great Hall which is a reproduction of an Elizabethan manor house in Berkshire,
England. The seven exterior chimneys serve 11 fireplaces in the house.

Special amenities: State-of-the-art stereo system,
concealed projection screen.

Additional highlights: Located 35 miles north of
Chicago, this is one of Lake Forest's finest older
estates. The extensive park-like grounds have been
redefined by Boston landscape architect Peter
Cummin who, in addition to sculpting the woodlands, re-established the original pond and
orchards. Today, the estate shows to perfection
inside and out.

OPPOSITE: *The Great Hall, a reproduction of an Elizabethan manor house located
in Berkshire, England, was added to the estate in the 1930s by architects Wolcott &
Work. Features include fossil tile flooring, a marble-encased fireplace, and a loft that
acts as both a passage and a gallery from which to view the artwork in the room.*
TOP: *From its oak-pegged hardwood floor to its fireplace with marble surround, the
living room suggests a level of elegance ideal for entertaining. The oak beams that
cross the ceiling are baronial without being overbearing.* ABOVE: *Custom book-
shelves and a fireplace are among the library's appointments.*

Large bay windows were positioned to face south and west, exposing open views of the landscape and bringing in some much-needed light. Decorative alterations allowed for lighter woodwork and softly textured glazed walls, both proving to complement the owner's fine collection of antiques and 20th century art. New bathrooms, kitchen and pantry areas, and a wine cellar were all worked into the design along with updated mechanical and electrical systems.

The landscape architect, Peter Cummin, was an equal partner in this endeavor. He and his Boston-based team worked hand-in-hand with the owners and David Easton

ABOVE: *A sizeable orchard contributes to the park-like ambience of the estate's 33 acres.* OPPOSITE TOP: *The main entrance to Derwen Mawr.* OPPOSITE BOTTOM: *Part of the property's renovation in the 1980s included the restoration of the grounds to their 1920s splendor. Among landscape architect Peter Cummin's achievements were the sculpting of the woodlands, the re-establishment of the estate's original pond, and the fashioning of new entry gates.*

to devise a plan that would bring complete harmony to the house and its setting. While thoughtfully considering the orientation and the history of Derwen Mawr, Mr. Cummin went on to cultivate vistas throughout the property, design a new terrace with pool for the guest house, fashion new entry gates, entry drive and courtyard, and, finally, carve out a pond to the west. At every point in this collaboration, the emphasis was on maintaining the dignity and integrity of the home, while allowing it to function as beautifully in the present as it had during the time of Mr. and Mrs. Jones.

Happily, all the wonderful old brickwork patterns can

still be seen rising from ground level to the chimneytops— all seven of them, which serve a total of 11 fireplaces. And the sun dial set into the brickwork above the front door remains. It was Mr. Jones who placed it there, always maintaining that it kept very good time. It might be said that the home he built some 70 years ago, Derwen Mawr, has kept very good time as well.

Photography by Bill Crofton.

Derwen Mawr was presented in Unique Homes by Genevieve Plamondon, Koenig & Strey, Lake Forest, IL.

Las Urracas

In the Tesuque Valley near Santa Fe, New Mexico

When a Los Angeles-based real estate consultant and writer came with his family to Santa Fe in 1987, they, like the Indians centuries before them, discovered one of the great natural treasures of the Southwest, located less than 10 minutes north of town. It is here, where the Tesuque River traces a lush alluvial soil valley, that the region briefly forgets its sunbaked landscape and the rich soil fosters grassy plains, bowers of deciduous trees and running waters. The miniature village of Tesuque, comprised of a post office, school, general store, restaurant and not much else, is rimmed by Indian and National Forest lands. The Sangre de Christo range rises in the distance.

"We were inescapably inspired by the sun, the land and the views," maintains the owner, who has lived and worked in countless cities from Philadelphia to Pasadena. "And we were most fortunate in our choice of John Midyette as our architect." Midyette is perhaps best known for his work as project captain for the rebuilding of the Santa Fe Opera complex after it burned down 25 years ago. "He has a phenomenal design sense, and he worked very hard at getting to know us as intimately as possible," says the owner admiringly. The result is a home that perfectly mirrors the attitudes and aesthetics of the people who live there. And it is a home that has clearly found its spirit in this time-honored land of northern New Mexico.

OPPOSITE TOP: *A private oasis in the Southwestern desert, this estate offers the rare combination of grassy meadows, deciduous trees, river frontage and mountain views, all only minutes from the center of Santa Fe.* OPPOSITE BOTTOM: *The Tesuque River runs through the property close to the main house.* ABOVE: *Set apart from the main residence is this guest house/office of approximately 2,600 square feet.* LEFT: *A six-stall barn, corral, arena for dressage and jumping, and easy access to an extensive network of riding trails make this an excellent property for the serious equestrian. In the background is the adobe main house, designed by architect John Midyette in the traditional pueblo style.*

LEFT: *The dining room affords an ambience that is classic Santa Fe. Here, flooring of Saltillo tile laid in a checkerboard fashion abuts floorboards of alternating white oak and walnut.* BELOW LEFT: *In the kitchen, modern conveniences and handsome wood cabinetry have been successfully integrated into a space defined by vigas, plastered adobe walls and curving archways.* BELOW: *A carved horse's head adorns the newel post at the base of the staircase leading to the second floor.*

On a verdant 12 acres, the compound previously owned by art dealer Gerald Peters still retains the guest house, but the main residence is all new and according to its owner, "built to look like it's been here forever." Legend has it that in these parts, all roads lead to Chaco Canyon, and here the owners borrowed on the traditions of the Pueblo Bonito; the swells and curves of every surface are pure adobe. In fact, there's only one right angle in the whole house; given the beams, square-cut tiles, two-by-fours and such, this was no small feat.

Where there is not gleaming Saltillo tile laid in checkerboard fashion, the floors are of unsteamed walnut (the steaming process is commonly done to minimize irregularities in the wood), Brazilian cherry and striped patterning of white oak and walnut. The vigas, beams and plastered adobe walls are pure Santa Fe, but many of the fixtures—lanterns, columns, tabletops, etc.—were brought from Mexico. As the owner tells it: "The Midyettes joined my wife and I on a little trip to Guadalajara. We discovered this dusty old antique shop, and many margueritas later, we came home with half the store!" The massive wrought iron chandelier that now

hangs in the foyer was one of their most rewarding finds. "We knew it would either be perfect or completely wrong. It was more than perfect!"

Through plastered archways and windows framed in stained pine, a scene of desert sky, flowers, leafy trees, grass and grazing horses unfolds, with the constant sound of river water in the background. The owner works out of an office/guest house well removed from the main residence, a wonderful spot for gazing out at the magpies from which the property takes its name. His wife and daughter practice their dressage and jumping near the stables and corral out back. And a few feet beneath the riding ring is an ancient burial ground. In their ceremonies for the dead, the Indians smashed pottery on the graves, and countless shards are still collected here today.

When asked if he felt this was all a bit unsettling, the owner merely replied, "Not at all. The Tesuque land is all about regeneration."

Photography by Chris Corrie and Murrae Haynes.

Las Urracas was presented in Unique Homes by Santa Fe Properties, Santa Fe, NM.

LEFT: *Decorative columns brought from Mexico support intricately carved ceiling beams and flank the approach to the step-up living room.* BELOW LEFT: *A sitting area, featuring large windows with views of the surrounding grounds, a fireplace and Saltillo tile flooring, adjoins the kitchen to create an enormous area for family living and dining.* BELOW: *Among the distinctive appointments in the foyer are the massive wooden double entry doors and the chandelier which the owners discovered in an antique shop in Mexico.*

CHARACTERISTICS

Property size: 12 acres with river frontage in a rare alluvial soil valley within five minutes of Santa Fe.

Architectural style: Classic pueblo-style adobe compound.

When built: 1989-1990.

Square footage: 7,500.

Number of bedrooms: Four.

Number of baths: Five.

Outbuildings: 2,600-square-foot guest house/office set apart from main house, six-stall barn.

Distinctive features: Ingenious design incorporating hand-carved beams, tile work, vigas, plastered adobe walls and high ceilings. Light fixtures and columns brought from Mexico. Layout includes an in-home office, in-law quarters, children's play wing, and second-story master bedroom with sitting room and huge deck. In addition to the horse barn, equestrian facilities include a corral and arena for dressage and jumping.

Additional highlights: Wonderful river and mountain views. One of only a handful of properties in the area offering substantial acreage amid such a verdant setting. Complete privacy and flexibility in a home that is equally oriented to family, entertaining and business needs.

Desert Jewel

Paradise Valley, Arizona

From the east, the sun rises over the McDowell Mountains and enters in through seamless walls of glass, filling the interior of this Southwestern contemporary retreat with pure desert light. At sunset, to the west, the haunting image of the mysterious rock formation known as Praying Monk lingers in the purple shadows on Camelback Mountain. The verdant land that lies in between is known as Paradise Valley, a chosen spot that achieved township only 30 years ago, but has always been treasured for its striking beauty in the Arizona desert.

Iron gates framed in blossoms of oleander open to this expressive home, where Canadian architect Jack Long has mastered a rich dialogue of native design. In ancient times, Pueblo Indians gathered for ceremonial purposes in a large sunken structure

ABOVE: *Viewed through an uninterrupted wall of glass is the heart of the living space, including the columned "kiva" room. In the foreground is the reflecting pool which stretches from the fountain to the pool and spa.* LEFT: *The sunken championship tennis court, the valley's finest, is built on a lower level than the pool area and includes a viewing area and state-of-the-art night lighting.*

known as a kiva. Drawing on this ancient architectural design for inspiration, Long created, as the thematic center of the house, a sunken space—a "kiva" room—off of which the flanking wings reach outward with softly arched hallways and soothing down-lighting. Tongue-and-groove ceilings, cedar latillas, Saltillo tile floors and arching oak doors pay homage to the ancient craft of the Southwest. Contemporary elements fit neatly in concert, from the polished surfaces of brass, lacquer and oak, to the uninterrupted walls of glass.

Spanning nearly 9,000 square feet beneath extended rooflines and cedar ceilings, Long's design embraces a wonderful mix of open and private spaces, and all reach beyond to the sun and sky. Thirty feet up, a copper pyramid crowns the columned kiva. A wall of glass opens the morning room to the patio. The entertainment room with its oak-edged bar overlooks a sunken championship tennis court. The master suite—a home unto itself with gallery, sitting room, library, bedroom, steam room and two baths—culminates in its own private garden. At the

center of the U-shaped residence and accessible from virtually every space, the courtyard offers a flower-filled approach to the fountain, pool and spa waters.

Whether indoors or out, one is awed by the artistry and appropriateness of the design, as well as by the many high-tech attributes which are not as immediately obvious. Take, for instance, the movie projector screen, discreetly hidden within an Omega track lighting system. Not to be overlooked is the kitchen, where every amenity for five-star cuisine is neatly housed amid the finest European cabinetry and a clean sweep of Corian. Lending ease to all manners of entertaining are kitchen/bar facilities in the butler's kitchen and the entertainment room.

Few will ever experience a home so articulate in design, elaborate in detail, and yet so joyously liveable.

Photography by Don Giannatti.

Desert Jewel was presented in Unique Homes by Evan Katz, The Prudential Arizona Realty, Phoenix, AZ.

CHARACTERISTICS

Property size: Nearly six level acres.
Architectural style: Southwestern contemporary.
Square footage: 8,916.
Number of bedrooms: Three.
Number of baths: Four and one-half.
Distinctive features: Myriad Southwestern details such as cedar latillas and a central "kiva" room opening to the fountained courtyard and pool area, Saltillo tile floors throughout, glass doors opening to patios from nearly every room, top-grade chef's kitchen, seamless window walls, accents of oak and brass.
Additional highlights: Sunken championship tennis court with spectator area and state-of-the-art lighting for nighttime play.

ABOVE: *The wings of the home embrace the serene courtyard. Complete with swimming pool, spa and reflecting pool flanked by Saltillo tile planters, this area extends the living space outdoors and affords an ideal backdrop for large gatherings.* RIGHT: *The kiva room is two steps down from the entry level, and its ceiling rises some 30 feet to the soaring point of a copper pyramid. Four rounded pillars add to the drama.*

Château de Forêt

Vail, Colorado

It was mid-October of 1987 when developer Ron Byrne was thinking about putting some of his money into the stock market rather than into real estate. His wife, Paula, advised him to stick with what he knew best. A week later, the market crashed and Ron Byrne, unlike many others, was still sleeping soundly at night. A transplanted developer from Michigan, Ron came to Vail in 1978, skied every day for a year, and decided he somehow had to find a way of making a living here. As with comparable playgrounds of the monied and mobile such as St. Moritz, Monte Carlo and Marbella, the climate was recession-proof, and the setting itself, a treasure. It is a location that can never be duplicated...there is simply no land left.

Here amid the alpenglow of the Gore Range, just below Bear Tree ski run and overlooking the lights of Vail village, Byrne has created a home that clearly bespeaks his own unabashed credo on building: "I don't make any decisions based on economics." The 6,000-square-foot Bavarian chalet, where windows seem to reach out over the mountaintops, has recently sold, setting a new record for real estate prices in Vail. And, it is the result of just one of the 20 or so limited partnerships Byrne has enjoyed in his 14 years in this world-class resort community.

According to Byrne, "Return on investment is important, but I feel a high return on enjoyment is the key. Just how much do you think a person who makes millions values

OPPOSITE TOP & ABOVE: *From its stunning architecture and choice location just below the Bear Tree ski run, to its long list of amenities which even includes a heated driveway for wintertime ease, Château de Forêt is undoubtedly Vail's premier luxury residence.* OPPOSITE BOTTOM: *A full wall of windows framing a magnificent panorama of mountains and village lights, a soaring beamed ceiling and an inviting fireplace are among the appointments that make the living room as elegant as it is romantic.*

his only time away from work?" At Château de Forêt, Byrne has answered his own question. After skiing all day, the elevator is a nice touch. So, too, is the Infinity spa in the master bathroom. This is not a place where you devote winter mornings to plowing last night's snowfall. You don't have to; the driveway is heated, as are the 2,000 square feet of stone terraces encircling the home.

Half a million dollars in furnishings and accessories were selected for use in the house upon its completion in February of 1991. Among them were voluminous vel-

vet drapes, Icelandic sheepskin carpets, Irish linen pillows and European antiques upholstered in leather, tapestry and crewel. Thick terry cloth towels bearing the Château de Forêt monogram were hung in the baths, candles were set on the dining room table and a decanter of fine brandy was placed by the fire. Byrne makes everything as effortless and turnkey as possible. "We always have four or five projects going on and three warehouses full of furniture," he says, "not to mention hundreds of antique books."

OPPOSITE TOP: *From throughout Château de Forêt, the views of the majestic Gore Range are breathtaking, especially at sunset, when the fiery alpenglow gently fades to soothing pastels, ultimately yielding to the night lights from the village below.* INSET: *One of the home's hallmarks is the successful blending of fabrics and furnishings, as seen here in one of the six bedrooms.* TOP: *The library, with its overstuffed furnishings and cozy surroundings, is the perfect spot to spend a quiet afternoon with a good book.* ABOVE: *The kitchen was planned with the gourmet chef in mind.*

RIGHT: *Warmly appointed with paneled wainscoting and ceiling beams, the formal dining room opens through French doors to a spacious heated stone terrace with unobstructed views of the Gore Range.* BELOW: *Mountain scenery forms a magnificent backdrop in the master suite, which features its own stone terrace, a soaring ceiling and handsome fireplace.* OPPOSITE TOP: *The living room is a welcoming space, ideal for entertaining any time of the year.* OPPOSITE BOTTOM: *The master bath is lavishly equipped with a Jacuzzi tub and an oversized steam shower.*

CHARACTERISTICS

Property size: Approximately one-half acre.
Architectural style: Contemporary Bavarian chalet.
When built: Completed in 1991.
Number of rooms: 12.
Square footage: 6,000±.
Number of bedrooms: Six.
Number of baths: Six and one-half.
Distinctive features: Beautiful oak floors, soaring windows to capture views, high vaulted ceilings, custom furnishings and heated marble floors.
Special amenities: Catering-capacity kitchen with Thermodore appliances, Infinity spa in master bath, elevator, elaborate security and temperature-sensor systems, heated stone terraces and heated driveway.
Additional highlights: The most elaborate house ever built in Vail. Situated to capture views of the village, Gore Range and Bear Tree ski run.

But for all its opulent detail, the house has been carefully created to exude a warm, age-old European flavor. Buttery oak floors, brass Italian bath fixtures, thick curtains and balloon shades opening to an awesome alpine view make the residence as cozy and complete as can be. Moreover, Château de Forêt is very much at home in Vail, where the celebrities keep a profile far lower than their vaulted ceilings and the good life is more about family fun than about high finance and foie gras.

"Just being able to develop on the highest end of the market, where there are truly no limits as to what one creates, is what's so wonderful about what I do," explains Byrne. "And when you're working with this calibre of clientele, no one's ever under duress." It's a very privileged place to be...creating homes for some of the most interesting people in the world, in a place where leisure has no limits.

Photography by Tim Hébert, Vail, CO, (c)1991.

Château de Forêt was presented in Unique Homes by Ron Byrne & Associates Real Estate, Vail, CO.

House-on-Hill

Hillsborough, California

In the gallery, the floor is marble, laid without mortar, point to point, to create a deep pattern of optical illusion. The walls are dowell-joined Jacobean panelling, purchased through Stair and Andrew in London. Eighteenth-century English oak surrounds the gentleman's cloak room, where special shallow cupboards were fashioned to hold shaving mugs. For the master sitting room, the owner and architect chose oak paneling, circa 1724, from Royal House Cononley; and the chandelier, constructed a few years later, is Waterford, purchased from a descendant of the actor Edmund Kean. Pine carving attributed to Grinling Gibbons, woodcarver to St. Paul's Cathedral under Sir Christopher Wren, and matching 18th century pine bookcases grace the library, featured in Helen Comstock's *100 Most Beautiful Rooms in America*.

For more than 60 years, the Hillsborough mansion with the unassuming name "House-on-Hill" has been cited as one of the most spectacular private residences ever created, and one that is certainly without peer in its fine antique English style. In the 1920s, Mrs. Tobin Clark, an heiress to the Hibernia Bank fortune, commissioned architect David Adler to create a Cotswold Tudor

ABOVE: *The cloistered loggia adjoins a large central court. As this area adjoins the main entertaining rooms of the residence, it is well positioned for outdoor entertaining on a grand scale.*
RIGHT: *The unusual Cotswold facade of House-on-Hill is considered a masterpiece and represents the most enduring work of architect David Adler. Entirely hand-built, the home was constructed from 1929 to 1931.*

mansion on a secluded hilltop of some 400 acres just south of San Francisco. Full-grown trees were transplanted from as far away as the Monterey Peninsula, rose terraces and formal courtyards were laid out amid the oak groves and lawns, and multiple-trunked olive trees were pruned to dip low over matching reflecting pools set in a stone terrace. Completely by hand, an architectural treasure was built—all mellowed brick, Carmel stone and half timbers on the outside, with 35,000 square feet of honey-colored woods, silver, crystal, leaded glass and 400-year-old parquetry on the inside.

It has been written that for several years prior to building the mansion, Mrs. Clark had been collecting ideas, clippings, photographs and other inspirations for her home. And it is known that during its somewhat lengthy construction, the estate pulled many local laborers and one failing planing mill right through the Depression. In two years alone, more than one million dollars was poured into the local economy, and at least three area firms were spared from bankruptcy.

OPPOSITE: *Colorful flower gardens and a large terrace accentuate the swimming pool. Immediately adjacent is a stone and brick cabana.* TOP: *A view across the rear lawn to rolling hillsides beyond.* ABOVE: *The main drive leads past hedges and rolling lawns before passing through stone pillars to an expansive motor court.*

ABOVE: *Flanked by marble fireplaces and floored in antique parquetry from Europe, the drawing room has been host to some of the Peninsula's most lavish social events over the years.* OPPOSITE TOP: *The library has been called "One of the 100 most beautiful rooms in America."* OPPOSITE BOTTOM: *The walls of the reception hall are lined with 17th century Jacobean oak paneling.*

Upon completion in 1931, the home was filled with interior decor by Syrie Maugham (wife of Somerset), paintings by Van Dyke and Sir Joshua Reynolds, Queen Anne paneling, 18th century Chinese wall coverings, a rare Dubois writing table and over 200 other items sent from England and the Continent. In the first gala she hosted at House-on-Hill, Mrs. Clark hired the Pro Arte Quartet of Brussels to play in the 55-foot grand salon. One subsequent autumn evening, two baffled journalists, who mistakingly had been sent by LIFE magazine to do a feature on the "typical" American home, arrived to find a busy staff preparing for a private concert that was to be given that night by the Budapest String Quartet.

Nothing ordinary happened here, even in the kitchen which, it has been written, "was inviolate except to the cook, who presented meals with the help of a two-story pantry and walk-in silver vault, with daily menus hand-lettered in French by the butler." Many today still remember the night when Karine Albert, Mrs. Clark's granddaughter, made her debut into society. Hundreds of guests were surrounded in a scene of Elizabethan finery, complete with verdant swags of ivy, sculpted topiary, pillars trailing satin ribbons and heraldic devices, wines from the estate cellar and food which this night, like any

other, was nothing less than superb. It was considered the party of the decade.

Though it has been more than 25 years since Mrs. Tobin Clark's death, the estate still exudes a spectacular energy and elegance. Walking through the 30-room interior with its 11 fireplaces, sitting beneath the archways of the loggia, strolling about the gardens or basking by the pool, one is awed by the decades of labor and love devoted to the estate. It has been called a "priceless monument to the better things in life."

With a prized view overlooking San Francisco's Lower Bay and the rolling landscape far to the west, House-on-Hill now rests on a more manageable six acres, without the original Adler-designed 16-stall stables, 10-car garage and "laundry group." Little else, though, has been sacrificed, and the house remains quietly tucked away behind the espaliered magnolias and majestic pines of a cherished Hillsborough setting.

Photography by Leslie Venners, The Iris Group.

House-on-Hill was presented in Unique Homes by Francis Hunter and Pat Kiisk, Fox & Carskadon/Better Homes and Gardens, San Mateo, CA.

🏛

CHARACTERISTICS

Property size: Approximately six acres.
Architectural style: Cotswald Tudor manor.
When built: 1929-1931.
Number of rooms: Approximately 30.
Square footage: 35,000.
Outbuildings: Poolside cabana, gardener's cottage and three-car garage.
Distinctive architectural details: Museum-quality features include 17th century oak Jacobean paneling, carvings attributed to Grinling Gibbons, 400-year-old parquetry and trompe l'oeil marble floors.
Additional highlights: Considered "one of America's last great homes," this mansion by David Adler rests on a portion of an original 35,000-acre Spanish land grant. Today the property offers magnificent gardens with statuary and fountains, a swimming pool, landscaped walkways, automatic irrigation, gated enrance and 360° security fencing.

A Landmark Afloat

Sausalito, California

Like its namesake palace in Agra, this floating "Taj Mahal" features desert-white towers, onion domes and ogee arches rising ceremoniously toward the heavens. The intricately carved fascia above the entrance is a replica of the portal at the original Taj Mahal, and sliding panels of grille-work on the windows permit privacy while patterning the walls and floors with mysterious weavings of sunlight and shadow. This Taj Mahal is, in fact, a floating palace of Mogul and Moorish influences presiding nobly over a long boardwalk at Dock One in Sausalito. In 1984, *House and Garden* wrote: "One's first view of the Taj...resembles the lengthy approach to the famous mausoleum in Agra. The difference is salt air and surreal presence of the bobbing bowsprits of the sailboats flanking the pier. They seem to be at once nodding and bowing while forming an arched canopy in deference to their master."

The master here is a San Francisco-based developer who calls his home a "mood elevator." He has lived on the water all his life, and prior to launching into this project, he actually spent some time in the Vale of Kashmir, immersing himself in the houseboat way of life typical of Dal Lake.

Several years and twice as many design consultants later, the houseboat the *San Francisco Chronicle* described as having "all the comforts of a landmark edifice...but near better restaurants," was at last completed.

Within the three-story interior are living and dining rooms, two kitchens, an elevator, wine cellar, elegant staterooms along with a silk-draped master suite, and an open upper-level pavilion designed to capitalize on the views. There's the casual camaraderie of dockside just below, a wide vista of the bay, the rambling hills of Sausalito, Belvedere Island, Mt. Tamalpais and more. And, it's just 12 minutes from the office in San Francisco.

While indoors a palette of cool white-to-beige travertine and monochromatic tones prevails, the owner explains, "Here I'm surrounded by colors in constant change...the

LEFT: *This houseboat's unique blend of Mogul and Moorish architecture—complete with onion domes and carved archways—gives it a commanding presence as it floats majestically in its kingdom at Sausalito's Dock One.* ABOVE: *San Francisco Bay is the colorful backdrop for this one-of-a-kind residence. In addition to fabulous views in all directions, the home offers dockage for two yachts of up to 70 feet and is accessible by seaplane.*

🏛

CHARACTERISTICS

Architectural style: Three-level houseboat with Mogul and Moorish influences.

When built: 1980s.

Square footage: Approximately 4,500.

Number of bedrooms: Four staterooms.

Number of bathrooms: Four.

Distinctive features: Largely inspired by the Taj Mahal, the home is a floating white palace filled with arched portals, latticed windows, open pavilion and deck areas, and a roofline distinguished by two onion domes. Four fireplaces, two kitchens (one gas, one electric), elevator, marble-floored bar opening to deck, silk-upholstered master suite, captain's library, spa tub and sauna, extensive built-in systems including radiant floor heat, stereo, fire and security. Can be divided into two separate quarters.

Additional highlights: "Anchorage" includes portside and starboard-side berths (each 70 feet); 360-degree views from most exclusive dock site in Sausalito. Panorama includes Sausalito Hills, Mt. Tamalpais, Belvedere Island and San Francisco (12 minutes away).

TOP: *Turkish rugs and saddlebags add a splash of color to the top deck.* ABOVE: *In the living room, beautifully sculptured grilles function as window screens to shield the sun, provide privacy (they also work as sliding panels) and create rich patterns of light.* OPPOSITE: *The high-ceilinged living room opens through a series of archways to a marble deck overlooking the ever-changing activity on San Francisco Bay.*

birds, the boats, the sailors passing by. I felt a backdrop of shades of white would glow and illuminate the blues of the bay, the greens of the hills, and the flowers and people within."

Mogul custom dictates interiors abounding with multicolored carpets and intricate inlaid walls and furnishings. But in this palace, the sparseness is an asset. There is sun and wind and sea and sky, and these elements are indeed decoration enough.

The owner has concluded that because most people aren't used to being on a houseboat, it brings out the best in them. "It's unique," he says, "a folly. And we just don't have enough follies in life."

Photography by Charles White.

The "Taj" was presented in Unique Homes by Gardner Mein and Janice Shaver, Grubb & Ellis Real Estate, San Francisco, CA.

Villa Lauriston

Portola Valley, California

Following the San Francisco earthquake of 1906 and the devastations brought on by subsequent fires, The Committee of 50—a group of philanthropic men who took on the monumental job of rebuilding San Francisco from the ground up—was formed. Among the distinguished committee members was Herbert E. Law, a real estate titan who commandeered reconstruction of the city's public transportation and sewer systems as well as the resurrection of his own Fairmont Hotel, which he and his brother had acquired literally hours before the earthquake. One year later, not only was it the first of the grand hotels to re-open, it was more opulent than ever following Law's $1.8 million gutting and rebuilding.

Some 15 years later it was Herbert Law's own home that captured headlines throughout northern California. After making his fortune patenting a medicine known as Viavi, a homeopathic cure for a host of ailments unique

OPPOSITE TOP: *Per Herbert Law's wishes, Villa Lauriston was created to emulate the essence and feel of a Florentine villa without being a copy of any other structure.* OPPOSITE BOTTOM: *The view over the pool by day.* ABOVE: *The nighttime spectacle afforded by the villa.*

CHARACTERISTICS

Property size: Nearly 21 acres.
Architectural style: Florentine villa.
When built: 1922-1926. Renovations throughout the 1980s.
Number of rooms: 20.
Square footage: 13,000±.
Number of bedrooms: Seven.
Number of bathrooms: 10.
Distinctive features: 18-foot-high hand-painted ceilings, Venetian frescoes, elaborate surfaces of marble and onyx, rich cherry and walnut paneling, many fittings brought from older mansions in the San Francisco area as well as churches and palaces in Europe.

to women, and after a sordid scandal involving a 25-year-old school teacher, Law finally settled down to the business of creating a proper home with a proper wife in Portola Valley, about an hour's drive north of San Francisco. This was the beginning of the legend known as Villa Lauriston.

In 1922, Law and his new wife began supervising the four-year creation of a Florentine-style villa that would eventually include seven bedrooms, 10 bathrooms, 10 fireplaces, fabulous marble columns and floors brought from Italy, and a glass conservatory purchased from the estate of one of San Francisco's founders. A railroad was built to transport raw native sandstone to the construction site, and a labyrinth of tunnels was blasted in order to facilitate building the foundation for the 13,000-square-foot residence. The hundreds of workers Law employed fitted precious marbles, wood paneling and

OPPOSITE: *The music room has a secret panel which opens to a staircase leading to the private rooms above.* LEFT: *In the formal dining room, tall arched windows frame a panoramic eastern view of San Francisco Bay.* BOTTOM LEFT: *Marble and stone fountains abound throughout the villa's grounds.* BELOW: *The foyer immediately sets a tone of formal elegance with its two ancient breccia marble columns, flooring of polished black Belgian and white Carrara marble, leaded glass windows and the intricately carved oak door and wood grille found at the entrance to the Grand Hall.*

massive wrought iron by day; at night they camped out in tents on these very grounds some 1,350 feet above San Francisco Bay.

A keen and creative gardener who, on his former estate, cultivated beladonna, marijuana and other secret herbs for the Viavi cure, Law was no less lavish in his plans for the grounds of Villa Lauriston, which in his day spread across 600 acres near Menlo Park. Today, the property of nearly 21 acres is adorned with a magnificent dolphin fountain at the entrance, a beautiful reflecting pool, swimming pool and spa, marble and stone fountains positioned about the grounds, a fish pond, and elegant statuary overseeing the gardens. All this awaits at the end of an entrance drive that spans two and a half miles; it is also at the heart of 1,000 acres of protected open space.

Over the past 70 years, Villa Lauriston has been home to a host of interesting owners, among them the personal attorney and confidant of William Randolph Hearst; a Japanese industrialist who is said to have lived in the home only a few weeks a year (though he kept it fully staffed at all times); and a former mayor of Manila who, yet another previous owner maintains, used to hang his washing out on the flagpole.

For over a decade, however, the present owners have devoted all their time, care and attention to the restoration and beautification of Herbert Law's dream. And, once again, it is considered among the most magnificent private estates in all of America.

Photography by Leslie Venners, the Iris Group.

Villa Lauriston was presented in Unique Homes by Barbara Tyler and Scott Dancer, Grubb & Ellis, Menlo Park, CA.

Il Paradiso

Montecito, California

CHARACTERISTICS

Property size: Three acres.
Architectural style: Italian Renaissance villa.
Distinctive features: Terra cotta tiles and frescoes, 19th century Florentine and French Regency mirrors, silk-draped skylights, variegated travertine floors, formal balustrades and archways, massive 18th century French buffet in the dining room, and a loggia extending the full length of the house.
Additional highlights: Spectacular grounds include 50 olive trees, towering cypress trees, cutting gardens, fountains, and a "water staircase" descending to the Roman pool and pavilion with spa.

I f you haven't been to Montecito in a decade or so, it may be time for a second look. The move is on to bring back some of the lost lustre of the early days — Italian gardens, marble terraces, black tie galas, grand-scale villas and the like. And one of the most ardent supporters of Montecito's renaissance is Jon Sorrell, who ardently maintains, "Montecito is a classic Mediterranean community and should remain so."

Here in 1987, Sorrell and his wife, Annette, purchased an ocean-view house which had been built in the 1960s for a retired Air Force officer. What Sorrell envisioned, though, had little in common with the existing contemporary property, and so began the one and one-half year transformation of a home which would eventually be named "Il Paradiso."

ABOVE: *The living room displays the elegance of a grand salon.* RIGHT: *The view from the grand terrace.* OPPOSITE: *Il Paradiso was inspired by the work of 16th century architect Giacomo Vignola.*

Great admirers of the Italian architectural masters, specifically Palladio and Vignola, the Sorrells have made countless trips to Italy, studying classical buildings as well as purchasing antiques, art and artifacts. They've also brought back with them an understanding of why we keep returning to the past. Jon says, "We have revivals typically every 75 to 100 years with people rediscovering the classics. Even Vignola's work was only a revival and synthesis of earlier architectural forms, taking ideas from antiquity."

It was one of Giacomo Vignola's 16th century villas northwest of Rome that served as inspiration for the Sorrell's Montecito residence. Many similar materials were employed, including hand-formed terra cotta paving tiles and frescoes incorporated in the

ABOVE: *One of the estate's most beautiful features is the terraced water staircase which descends from the grand terrace to the pool.* OPPOSITE TOP: *Chandeliers adorn the main entry hall.* OPPOSITE BOTTOM: *Twin 400-foot driveways end in a 6,000-square-foot stone-paved motor court.*

plaster walls of the dining room. Tapestries and an oil canvas from the 17th century Seville Academy of Painting were chosen for the living room. Framed by Tuscan columns, the archways in the south-facing loggia open to a peerless view of the gardens to the sea.

Very much at one with its setting, the villa opens to grounds of period formality. Landscape architect Phil Shipley was commissioned to set the stage for a Renaissance villa complete with towering cypress trees, a carpet of white jasmine and creeping juniper, flower-filled pots beside the Roman pool, and a terraced water staircase fashioned after one at Villa Farnese, the home Vignola built for Cardinal Farnese four centuries ago. Next to the pool is a pavilion

designed in keeping with the style of the main house.

An architectural designer with a rather determined outlook on the future of Montecito, Jon Sorrell admits to being happiest when "undoing" the marginal and passe modern designs of recent years and concentrating on the Mediterranean elegance of Montecito in its heyday of the early 1900s.

He accomplishes this best when recreating homes that, when completed, seem to make us all aware that the centuries past need not be times forgotten.

Photography by Annette Sorrell.

"Il Paradiso" was presented in Unique Homes by Paul O'Keeffe, Joyce Gibb Realty, Santa Barbara, CA.

# of Beverly Hills
California ——————

This imposing mansion—reminiscent of the great chateaux of Europe—commands a setting of more than two acres at the end of a private mani-cured road in one of the world's most famous communities. Inside the gated entrance, the slate motor court can accommodate 50 cars.

BELOW: *The grand hall is overwhelming with its sweeping staircase and domed stained glass ceiling which supports an antique Italian chandelier weighing 6,000 pounds.* OPPOSITE TOP: *The rear facade overlooks a vast expanse of lawn as well as the estate's own putting green.* OPPOSITE BOTTOM: *The classical main entrance immediately sets a tone of unrivaled opulence and grandeur. Indicative of the world-class craftsmanship on display throughout the mansion are the 22-foot-high teak double front doors.*

It is difficult to exaggerate about a house spanning well over 40,000 square feet. In the case of this newly completed "chateau" in Beverly Hills, it is relatively impossible. For the owner and builder, Alexander Coler, the mansion on Shadow Hill serves as a living tribute to a life's work. A self-made success in commercial construction, the man who built the 3.5 million-square-foot Anaheim Hilton set out to build a home of his own in 1986, and in the next six years an address of inimitable grandeur evolved.

The "footprint" of the home measures approximately 15,000 square feet, with the upper and lower floors nearly tripling these proportions. "I don't think we had a crew of more than 30 or 40 working on the site at any one time," says Coler with a builder's matter-of-factness. But for a veteran in the industry, Coler (now in his seventies) even speaks with amazement about some of the challenges the project presented. The foyer's 40' x 50' leaded and stained glass ceiling—its central glass dome supporting a 6,000-pound brass chandelier—was one of them. The staircase beneath this glass ceiling, Coler adds, took over a year to build.

Inspired by the great chateaux of Europe, Coler envisioned a palace all his own, but one filled with light and open to the outdoors. The great sweep of the entry hall leads onto 1,500 square feet of marble terracing surrounding a magnificent fountain. Every room extends to a panorama of city, ocean and countryside. And in the case of the dining room, walls and floors visually defy their very boundaries. As 50 or more are seated for dinner, a hand-carved vaulted ceiling reigns overhead; meanwhile, the expanse of Lalique-patterned etched

ABOVE: *As handsome as it is functional, the gourmet kitchen is capable of handling the demands of grand-scale living and entertaining.* OPPOSITE TOP: *Towering marble columns, marble flooring and a fireplace with beautifully carved mantel are featured in the living room. Here, as is typical throughout, the use of large windows brings in an abundance of natural light.* OPPO-SITE BOTTOM: *Part of the 5,000-square-foot master suite, "her" bath includes a fireplace, marble floor, an elevated spa tub set into marble, and a marble shower.*

glass underfoot serves as a floor for the dining room and a ceiling for the indoor pool located one level below.

Though the home has yet to be lived in, it's had more than few opportunities to prove itself the perfect host. Several charity functions have been staged here, as was the wedding of actress Connie Sellecca to John Tesh. With private parking for more than 50 cars, a kitchen equipped with three dishwashers and a walk-in refrigerator, dumb-waiter and elevator service to each level, and a complete theatre/ballroom/casino complex on-site, the residence is as self-sufficient as virtually any four-star hotel.

The owner has also seen to a few personal pleasures, among them two regulation-size bowling lanes ("I thought my grandchildren would enjoy this, and maybe someday I'd have time to get good at the game, too."); and a master suite some 5,000 square feet in size. "Her" bath has its own fireplace; "his" comes with a Japanese soaking tub and spa. The bedroom, reached off a gallery rotunda, is just a few steps away from the home's own barber shop/beauty salon and exercise room with sauna.

Other amenities include a second banquet kitchen, vast wine cellar, eight-car garage, guest apartment, staff and chauffeur's quarters, and state-of-the-art systems for security and communications. In addition to 4,700

square feet of marble terraces, the 2.25-acre grounds include a tennis court cantilevered into a hillside—its projection supported by massive 50-foot beams to meet necessary earthquake requirements.

Of the house that took $20 million (exclusive of the land) and high-rise cranes to build, Alexander Coler is quietly proud. "I know what it's like to live in a 1,000-square-foot home," he recalls of the early years, "and we lived quite comfortably." After a lifetime of hard work, his labors are celebrated in an estate that is perhaps only rivaled in scope by "Graystone," the Beverly Hills home of the Doheny family. Mr. Coler coolly states, "I think it's a few thousand feet larger than mine." But there is no edge of envy in his voice. And there are clearly no regrets.

With all the temptations that await behind the massive 22-foot-high teak doors that open to his home, Alexander Coler admits he only has one favorite pastime: "Building."

Photography by Michael McCreary.

The Crown Jewel of Beverly Hills was presented in Unique Homes by Martin Geimer and Bernice Gershon, Coldwell Banker/Previews®, Beverly Hills, CA.

⚏ Characteristics

Property size: 2.25 acres.

Architectural style: French chateau.

When built: Begun in 1986.

Number of rooms: More than 45.

Square footage: 37,000+ (exclusive of terraces).

Number of bedrooms: Nine.

Number of baths: 13 full, seven half-baths.

Outbuildings: Eight-car garage with artist's studio.

Distinctive features: 4,700 square feet of marble terraces, 5,000-square-foot master suite, 3,600-square-foot ballroom, etched glass floors, stained glass ceilings, 22-foot teak entry doors, marble columns and flooring, a total of nine fireplaces, elevator and dumbwaiter service to all levels, and wonderful ocean and city views.

Additional highlights: Two tournament-certified bowling lanes, north/south tennis court, indoor swimming pool with etched glass ceiling above, in-house barber shop/beauty salon. Property has been featured on "Lifestyles of the Rich and Famous."

Sequestered in the Canyon

Santa Monica, California

ABOVE: *A slate motor court fronts this dramatic Mediterranean-style home, beautifully accentuated by nighttime lighting.* OPPOSITE: *The pool area, complete with waterfall and wonderful patio, provides access to a bath/changing room as well as a studio/guest room with private entry.*

The home lays upon a land that was the last hold on a Spanish grant dating back to 1769, at which time occupation of California was launched by Gaspar de Portola in San Diego. Its towering arches and beams recall the missions and presidios that followed the Spanish occupation. Its quiet echoes the stillness that lasted well into the 1800s, when Santa Monica remained no more than a whisper of unclaimed mesa covered with wild grasses. Now, as then, you can hear the ocean surf.

This Mediterranean estate is but minutes from the sea, yet tucked away in a place and time all its own— over a bridge that crosses a channel, beyond sheltering wrought iron gates, amidst flowers and falling waters,

and deep within the greenness of Santa Monica Canyon. The place has a wonderful sense of belonging, taking one back over a century ago when life in the canyon included, as one newspaper described it, "scenes of enchantment...thick clusters of bushes and trees, cool mountain water streams, beds of moss and ferns, shady nooks and tempting lovers' walks."

The European design of the home on Channel Road is credited to Mandel Development, an established high-end builder in the Los Angeles area, and a firm with an obvious eye for old world touches. A limestone-floored portico rising two stories high provides a sweeping approach to the 7,800-square-foot residence. The wrought iron entry door is classically Mediterranean; and just inside, the limestone continues

through a commanding vaulted entry.

Beams, arches and handsome stone hearths beautifully define the living space, with all modern luxuries (from Sub-Zero appliances to a sauna and spa in the master bath) comfortably fitting in. What you don't see are the behind-the-scenes workings of the home: central vacuum in every room, phone-linked security, and pre-wiring for computer, cable and stereo systems throughout.

Beyond these foot-thick walls, the house reaches out from beneath its handmade clay tile roof at every turn. The formal dining room opens onto an intimate patio. A gracious loggia captures views over the broad deck and beyond to the swimming pool and waterfall. The master suite leads onto a private deck, while another

bedroom has a wrought iron balcony all its own. The land rolls gently away to an expanse of grassy lawn where a tennis court is to be constructed. It's difficult to imagine Los Angeles lies practically next door.

In fact, big-city dwellers were the ones who put the canyon on the map back in the 1860s, coming here to escape the heat and the dust, pitching tents, lighting bonfires, holding Saturday night dances and enjoying all manner of merrymaking by the sea. No one seemed to have any doubt when the Los Angeles papers touted that a week here "would add 10 years to your life."

This estate was presented in Unique Homes by Bob Hurwitz, Hurwitz-James Company, Realtors, Los Angeles, CA.

CHARACTERISTICS

Property size: One-plus acre.

Architectural style: Contemporary Mediterranean.

Square footage: 7,800 ±.

Number of bedrooms: Six.

Number of baths: Eight.

Distinctive features: Limestone-floored portico, handmade clay tile roof, high beamed ceiling and stone-hearthed fireplace in step-down living room, private patio off dining room, 10-foot ceilings on upper level. Open-air loggia adjoining family room; 1,500-square-foot master suite with fireplace, sitting room and deck; loft overlooking main-level den/office. House is equipped with gourmet kitchen appliances, telephone system with security, and wiring for cable TV, computer equipment and stereo system.

Additional highlights: Bath/changing room for swimming pool, broad deck overlooking pool and waterfall, planned area for a north/south tennis court. A bridge crossing a channel leads to this gated estate with eight-car motor court and three-car garage, plus private guest suite with separate entrance.

OPPOSITE: *The estate viewed from the air.* ABOVE: *The tile-floored loggia off the family room overlooks the lush pool area.* RIGHT: *A beautifully crafted wrought iron door opens to the vaulted two-story entry, featuring limestone floor and sweeping staircase.* BELOW: *The family room/breakfast room/kitchen combination.*

On Lido Isle

Newport Beach, California

For 10 years, Bob and Lori Warmington have made their home in a French country house that was designed for their unique lifestyle...and theirs alone. Lori spends her days organizing new chapters of Grad Night Foundation, a high school drug and alcohol abuse program which began in California and, thanks to her efforts, now helps young adults from Virginia to Alaska. Bob, the originator and co-franchiser of Quality Suite and Comfort Suite Hotels, has overseen projects as broad in scope as the 4,000-acre Moreno Valley Ranch, and as personally gratifying as his own home in Newport Beach. Their professional pursuits leave little time for private pleasure, but when that moment comes, they're both headed home to Lido Isle and, once there, it's nothing but relaxation.

Together with Orange architect Aide Collie and Newport Beach interior designer Rose Evans, the Warmingtons created an architectural treasure amid 180-degree views of Newport Harbor's main channel, the islands of Newport Bay and the night lights of Fashion Island. Says Bob, "Here my wife can really enjoy some serenity and quiet, and escape her world of activity. Her favorite spot is a retreat in an ocean-view turret complete with a walk-in fireplace." Bob has his escape out

ABOVE: *Docking space for several large yachts and a sun-splashed bayfront terrace complement this prime setting on the tip of Lido Isle.* TOP RIGHT: *Trompe l'oeil wall paintings by noted artist Robert Jackson of New York and a grand curving staircase enhance the stately qualities of the entrance hall.* BOTTOM RIGHT: *Bay views form a panoramic backdrop to the elegance of the living room, complete with richly paneled walls and fireplace.*

RIGHT: *The turreted entrance facade, complete with entry doors imported from France, displays a European flair.* OPPOSITE TOP: *Views from the home encompass Newport Harbor's main channel and its islands. At night, the lights of Fashion Island add to the spectacle.* OPPOSITE BOTTOM: *A large picture window frames a stunning bay view in the bright and airy master bedroom.*

back—a boat neatly docked bayside, just a few feet from the waterfront terrace.

The 50-year-old builder and his wife have long been avid collectors of Impressionist art and antique furnishings. From dealers in both London and New York they've acquired some wonderful pieces from the Queen Anne period. "We specifically had this collection in mind when planning the house," explains Bob, "from the scale of each room to the picture-frame mouldings." He continues: "But we worked very hard at steering away from the museum look. It's so inapproachable, and that's not us." The views, the light, the buoyant colors all serve to make this an invitation to comfort.

Their home is also filled with great charm. The turret-topped entry doors are right out of a garden in Provence. In the living room, walls of walnut-stained alder wood are a golden amber by day and a deep whiskey color in the firelight. In the foyer, flowers and foliage reach indoors on the trompe l'oeil walls painted by Robert Jackson of New York. Other faux finishes by Jackson can be seen in New York's Metropolitan Museum of Art and at Blair House in Washington, D.C. Both Bob and Lori profess to being very visual people, and adamantly detail conscious. "No decorator makes any of these decisions," admits Bob. "This is purely our style."

The Lido Isle community has been a natural for the

CHARACTERISTICS

Property size: Oversized lot with 60 feet of bayfront.
Architectural style: Country French.
When built: 1983.
Number of rooms: 11.
Square footage: 6,500.
Number of bedrooms: Five.
Number of baths: Five.
Outbuildings: Three-car garage.
Distinctive features: Four fireplaces, gracefully curving staircase, parquet floors, ornate ceiling treatments, raised panel walls, generous windows to maximize views, slate roof.
Additional highlights: Spectacular 180-degree views from the tip of prestigious Lido Island, overlooking the harbor channel, lights of Newport Bay, and Fashion Island in the distance. Large dock, bayside terrace and spa are featured.

Warmingtons. It's all residential, enviably quiet and very oriented to the water, with more Bermuda shorts than black ties. Things tend also to be quite well-heeled, but, as Bob explains, they've made a conscious decision to hold back from the social circuit. "Though this is a great party house, we're really not into entertaining. We're very private people. Our best times are when the kids come home from college and fill the house with their friends." When you combine bare feet and Brunschwig fabrics with boating and a family dinner overlooking the bay, you get a glimpse of the style that Lori and Bob would call "approachable."

Photography by Tad Bonsall.

This Lido Isle residence was presented in Unique Homes by Coldwell Banker/Previews®, Newport Beach, CA.

OPPOSITE: *The library is crowned with a wood-paneled ceiling boasting massive beams. Also noteworthy is the leaded glass treatment in the top portion of the bay window, which overlooks the water.* LEFT: *Indicative of the home's superior craftsmanship is the paneled, arched passageway between the living room and the library.*

Camelot Comes to Fairbanks Ranch

Rancho Santa Fe, California

Y ou do not simply enter this magical estate. First, there are the massive wooden gates creaking as they open to your approach. Then, there is the moat to be crossed. Inside, the sound of footsteps is measured across distressed wood floors. Heralding your arrival is the trumpeting of horns...or is it just the imagination that has wandered back to the legendary world of Camelot?

The chateau is located in a time and place all its own, where birds soar over the turret top and waterfalls splash down rocky walls; where the scent is that of flowers and evening firesides, and light and laughter reach high into the trusses. It's the kind of place that takes lifetimes of dreams to create. A home where fairy tales live on.

The dream began a number of years ago when Ballard Smith and his wife, Charlie, took some time off to explore the French countryside, specifically the great chateaux of the wine region. They met up with houses centuries old and enduring as ever; homes which offered much inspiration for the place they would someday build for themselves. Eventually the Smiths found their chosen spot—a setting as personally rewarding as the residence they envisioned. The location was 120 miles south of Los Angeles in the gate-guarded confines of beautiful Fairbanks Ranch.

"We put our heads together with a local architect and builder," recalls Charlie Smith, who per-

OPPOSITE TOP: *From the rolling lawns that stretch to the private practice green, to the stone waterfalls cascading into the bass-stocked pond and the natural stone pool with built-in slide and grotto, this estate offers a truly special setting.* OPPOSITE BOTTOM: *The sprawling estate residence viewed from the air.* ABOVE: *This mansion was designed to epitomize the charms of the French countryside.*

sonally supervised the two-year project along with Russ McAvoy and Steve Sharratt of Sharratt Construction Company. Charlie adds, "In my opinion, this company is one of the finest builders in the San Diego area."

With no less determination and will than the mightiest of King Arthur's knights, Charlie and Ballard Smith researched their way through the centuries and lavished their home with all the regal touches. The fireplace in the great room was fashioned to fit snugly in a 15-foot wall of stone, proportionately balanced by trusswork rising more than 30 feet overhead. A few steps up, the billiards and gaming parlor, hushed in paneling from floor to ceiling, provided a handsome after-hours spot. The kitchen, though, was to be pure Provence, complete with two

LEFT: *Included in the estate's 3.6 acres is a guest house, pictured here. It includes one bedroom, a loft, a living room with stone fireplace, a dining room and full kitchen. The adjoining gazebo has a fully equipped wet bar, ideal for outdoor entertaining by the stocked pond and pool.* OPPOSITE: *The great room boasts a 32-foot-high ceiling.* BELOW: *The gallery hallway, ideal for displaying art, leads to the great room.* BOTTOM: *Adjoining the bedroom area of the master suite is a sitting area with fireplace, wet bar and outside access. Also included in the master suite are "his" and "her" baths, oversized closets, a private exercise room/gym with sauna and wet steam room, offices, a nursery and its own garage.*

stoves (one imported from France), a delightful breakfast room and connecting terrace with its own fireplace.

Trompe l'oeil ceilings soon rose above, custom carpets were laid underfoot and the massive front doors, beams, floors and cabinets were hand-milled on site. "I enjoyed selecting all the wallpaper and faux finishes which help complete the intricate touches that coax out the personality of the house," says Charlie. "Although the home is grandiose in size, one feels quite at home and comfortable here."

Indeed, comfort does prevail. In the dramatic gallery, an armored knight stands guarding his keep. Beyond is the master suite, occupying the south wing with its sitting and bedroom areas separated by a rich wood

BELOW: *Adjoining the great room is an elevated billiards/game room featuring a high ceiling, richly paneled walls and built-ins.*
BOTTOM: *"Her" master bath.* OPPOSITE: *The main living area of the house is centered around the great room. Among the appointments that distinguish this space are the fireplace set into a 15-foot stone wall, soaring ceiling beams, a full-service sit-down bar, and a bank of windows overlooking the grounds. A superb setting for evenings of memorable entertaining, this room also opens to the terrace, thus facilitating indoor/outdoor gatherings on a grand scale.*

balustrade. Adjacent are the owner's private offices, a nursery, steam room and private gymnasium. Another wing offers the children's bedrooms, convenient to a common study with its own phone booth.

Indoors, all is battened and beamed to perfection, with imported fixtures and fabric coverings bringing great color and light in the home. Outdoors, it is a fantasy of gardens, stone paths, grassy knolls and waterways meandering across three and one-half acres. The gazebo offers a choice view over a stocked bass pond. The enormous terrace overlooks a rock waterfall cascading into a grotto of blue pool waters. The separate guest house shares in the scene, but perhaps has the best outlook of all, for here you can take in all of the finery of a modern-day version of Camelot.

Photography by Ed Golich.

This fanciful estate was presented in Unique Homes by Else Fuller, Fairbanks Ranch Realty, a Division of The Prudential California Realty, Rancho Santa Fe, CA.

CHARACTERISTICS

Property size: More than three and one-half acres.

Architectural style: French country chateau.

When built: 1988 to 1990.

Number of bedrooms: Eight (exclusive of guest house).

Number of baths: 10.

Outbuildings: Full guest house, gazebo with bar.

Distinctive features: Domed trompe l'oeil ceilings, massive great room with 32-foot ceilings, six magnificent fireplaces (one is set in a 15-foot-high stone wall). Constructed on site were the huge front doors, tresses, beams, distressed wood floors and cabinetry. Superb kitchen wing includes breakfast room, terrace with fireplace and barbecue, butler's pantry and wine storage room. Master wing includes sitting area with fireplace and wet bar, separate garage, exercise room/gym with sauna, offices and nursery. Pool, stocked pond, tennis court and putting green included on the grounds.

Special amenities: Seven zones of heating and cooling, high-tech video and music systems, intercom system, elaborate security and lighting throughout.

Additional highlights: A one-of-a-kind showplace home in the prestigious gated community of Fairbanks Ranch, just minutes from five acclaimed golf courses and country clubs, Del Mar Race Track and the ocean.

Exclusive Irvine Cove Estate

Laguna Beach, California

The 48-foot solar-heated pool and spa plus wraparound loggias extend the living space outdoors, providing a dramatic backdrop for nighttime entertaining. OPPOSITE: *Irvine Cove*, enjoying a magnificent oceanfront location, is one of only a handful of communities in California that have state approval for private beach access.

nlike so many newer homes stacked up high on the Southern California coast, this sweeping, sun-filled residence conveys a sense of open, endless bounds. Walls seem to vanish as the outdoor areas reach in, and the horizon of ocean and sky brings in an awareness of endless dimensions. Once the showplace of a Chrysler Corporation executive, and more recently the private playground of a Saudi Prince, this Irvine Cove residence disposes of contemporary cliché while redefining modern elegance.

On the only double-lot property in this gate-guarded section of Laguna Beach, the home is a study in white against a sea of blue—its outspoken symmetry and hard-edge lines providing a stunning counterpoint to a

CHARACTERISTICS

Property size: Half-acre (double lot).
Architectural style: Pacific Coast contemporary.
Number of rooms: 15.
Square footage: 8,000.
Number of bedrooms: Six.
Number of baths: Six and one-half.
Distinctive features: Extensive use of marble, granite, golden tiling and hardwood, 25-foot-high ceiling in main reception area, stained glass window and hand-painted ceiling in master bath, all-new European kitchen.
Additional highlights: Four fireplaces, staff quarters with private entry, pool and spa accented by a life-size bronze palm tree fountain, lush tropical gardens and magnificent ocean views. One of the largest homes in gate-guarded Irvine Cove.

natural beach setting of cliffs and sand. Walls of glass, ceilings rising as high as 25 feet, lush garden views from every window, and private patios soften the cool expanses of marble and granite within the single-level design. In one grand and flowing gesture, the 8,000-square-foot interior opens onto a pool terrace with wraparound loggias and breezy palms. By day, this is the party-perfect setting with its Texas-size barbecue and large brick terrace. By night, all is magical and still in the reflections of moonlight.

The differing lifestyles and inherent demands of the home's two previous owners have, in many respects, contributed largely to the wonderful space and flexibility that have evolved here. Today, for instance, there are two distinct master suites, one opening to a fabulous bath where the huge spa tub is set beneath stained glass

ABOVE: *The sunny pool area comes complete with a large barbecue area for informal gatherings.* OPPOSITE TOP: *Fourteen-foot walls and a ceiling rising 25 feet over marble flooring set the stage for grand-scale events in the "Great Room."* OPPOSITE BOTTOM: *The European kitchen stands ready to meet all family and entertaining needs.*

windows and a hand-painted ceiling. The other is in a newer wing all its own, offering a separate living room, exercise room, kitchen area, office and private access to the pool.

There are places for personal family pleasure, such as the combined kitchen/family room overlooking the pool and spa, and settings of unabashed formality, including the "great room" where white marble floors, a marble bar and grand piano provide perfect accompaniment to an evening of elegance. In the all-new European kitchen every conceivable appliance plus gas and electric cooking centers stand ready to assist, whatever the occasion.

It is the easy and efficient array of systems, though, that makes this home most liveable. A projection screen quietly disappears into the ceiling in the living room. All the controls for household lighting are available at bed-

side. Stereo and television equipment is housed behind beautiful cabinetry. Automatic sprinklers tend to the palms and specimen plantings on the half-acre of grounds.

The myriad highlights of this home are only further distinguished by its surroundings: a residents-only beach right outside, some of the best fishing and sailing waters around, a charming town inspired by coastal European villages, and a community enriched with a host of artistic and cultural offerings. The setting and the home are indeed of very special privilege.

Photography by David Heath.

This estate was presented in Unique Homes by Shirley Harris, Coast Newport Properties, Newport Beach, CA.

Casa Isabella

Coronado, California

Garden paths wind their way through an Eden of bougainvillea, oleander, fan palms and wisteria. Malibu tiles line the fountains and planters with a host of floral motifs. The scents of sage and lavender carpet the walk to the front gate. From a deck on the rooftop, a view of blue unfolds, taking in the yacht club, the landmark bridge to San Diego and the beautiful Pacific. The scene is at once intimate and expansive, and quite typical of the great charm Coronado has held for well over a hundred years.

At Casa Isabella, it was Sheryll Jackman's goal to create a home nostalgic for the past, reflective of fine artistry, and yet engineered to literally think for itself. There are motorized awnings capable of sensing sun and rain, electronically controlled skylights, full exercise equipment hook-ups for an "at home" gym, and wardrobes and cabinets custom built to house everything from fine jewelry to a facsimile machine. These are

OPPOSITE TOP LEFT: *Night lighting accentuates the lush landscaping that is a hallmark of Casa Isabella.* OPPOSITE TOP RIGHT: *The intricate carving on the mahogany front door only hints at the level of craftsmanship awaiting within.* OPPOSITE BOTTOM: *This home exudes an aura of old world charm with its classic Spanish Colonial facade.* ABOVE: *The living room, featuring fireplace and mahogany ceiling, opens to a large water-view patio.* RIGHT: *An etched leaf pattern outlines the mirror and adds a distinctive touch to one of the two dressing rooms in the master suite.*

among the mechanics of the home that are well hidden from view.

What you do see, explains Sheryll, president of the Jackman Group, a multi-disciplinary design and construction firm based in Coronado, "is a comforting environment where people can escape and dream; a home that makes people feel good...that takes them away." The present owners of Casa Isabella come from a strong heritage of horticulture, and they commissioned the Jackman Group to integrate their love for all things that flower throughout the house. The front door of inlaid beveled glass is framed by a mahogany carving of 300 bougainvillea leaves with 80 blossoms. The hand-painted tiles are patterned with morning glories and wisteria. A dressing room mirror is etched in a leafy arbor design. One has the feeling of never having left the garden.

The extensive use of mahogany provides a gracious embellishment to the multi-level interior; for example, the mahogany cabinetry adorned with art glass which is on display in the living, dining and family rooms, the custom mahogany French doors featuring Conrad shades of natural grasses hand-woven in China, or the custom mahogany ceiling running through the living and dining

ABOVE: *Malibu tiles, hardwood flooring, lustrous cabinetry and commercial-grade appliances ensure a kitchen that is both handsome and functional.* OPPOSITE TOP: *The master bedroom is an elegant retreat with its vaulted ceiling, mahogany cabinetry and marble fireplace.* OPPOSITE BOTTOM: *Special features of the master bath include granite countertops, towel warmers, an oversized tub and a glass-enclosed shower.*

rooms. A vaulted mahogany ceiling and bow-front mahogany cabinetry may be found in the master bedroom, along with a travertine marble fireplace carved in a Spanish rope column motif that is similar to the design used in the dining room cabinetry.

Even the self-contained suite on the lower level exhibits a wealth of details and appointments: a full wall of mahogany built-ins, decorative tile in a morning glory pattern, a wet bar or kitchenette, and a humidity- and temperature-controlled rear closet with custom-designed spaces to accommodate everything from linens to rolls of gift paper.

"Today, more than ever before, people want things that are unusual and hard to find," says Sheryll. "They are searching for treasures and a little romance to indulge their spirit."

Given this philosophy, it is no wonder that Casa Isabella is such a rare find.

Photography by Kim Brun Studios, Inc.

Casa Isabella was presented in Unique Homes by Jack Lewis Realty, Coronado, CA.

CHARACTERISTICS

Architectural style: Spanish Colonial.
Distinctive features: Custom Malibu tiles, leaded art glass, carved mahogany doors, cabinets and ceilings, professional office, rooftop deck overlooking the Coronado Bridge and the Pacific Ocean.
Special amenities: State-of-the-art entertainment and security systems, elevator, Lutron scene-control lighting, master bath with three electronic skylights, towel warmers and built-in hairdryers.

Casa Palmilla

Los Cabos, Mexico

Beneath the archways of loggias peeking out to sea, beside the beach in one of the world's most inviting resort communities, basking in the sunshine of Baja California Sur, lies a villa poised on the edge of perfection. Cool tile floors, open-air verandas and vaulted ceilings are quite at home here in a village setting of cobblestone streets and the charms of Colonial Mexico. The 10,000-square-foot dwelling, the 1986 creation of architect Hugh Espinoza, is a fitting addition to the incomparable resort life of Los Cabos.

On a double-size lot fronting one of the peninsula's rare swimmable beaches, Casa Palmilla takes its name from the hotel that was once the private hideaway of such luminaries as Bing Crosby, John Wayne and President Dwight D. Eisenhower. In 1984, Hotel Palmilla was purchased by Donald M. Koll of Koll International, one of the largest real estate developers in the western United States; and today the Palmilla Resort spreads out across 900 acres on the eastern tip of the peninsula where the Sea of Cortez meets the Pacific.

A few minutes' walk from the hotel, this Spanish Colonial estate offers a rock-hugging territorial design built with a lot of pampering in mind. Bedroom suites are tucked away on each of three levels, with one afford-

OPPOSITE TOP: *The home's Spanish Colonial facade is reflected in the irregularly shaped pool, which is surrounded by a large patio set at the edge of the property overlooking the sandy beach.* OPPOSITE BOTTOM: *The dramatic coastline of Los Cabos affords a scenic backdrop for Casa Palmilla.* ABOVE & RIGHT: *Not only does the main veranda provide an expansive area for open-air living and entertaining, it affords a front-row view extending up and down the coast and out to the horizon over the Sea of Cortez.*

ing its own separate entrance, wet bar and private terrace. By contrast, entertaining areas flow easily into one another and beyond to the outdoors. At no time is one without a view to the sea. Also set against this horizon of blue is a pool terrace ideal for barbecues or dancing under the stars. The indulgences are many; the cares are few. And should you dare ask if the magic will ever end, the answer is always the same: mañana.

Integral to the rewards of Casa Palmilla are all the riches that await just a few steps away. There's sport fishing that rivals the finest waters in the world, especially if you're after the mighty marlin (though there are some 350 other species here, too). There's the best scuba diving in all of Mexico, with day and night dives supervised by certified instructors. Illuminated tennis courts as well as facilities for paddle tennis and croquet are nestled among tropical gardens. Horses are ready to take you out for a morning gallop on Playa Palma's two-mile stretch of sand. This is only a partial list of all that has earned Palmilla the title of "Best of the Best" of beachfront hotels in Latin America.

Yet for many, the main event here is sure to be Jack Nicklaus' 30-year dream come true. "Many people have approached me regarding designing courses in Mexico,"

ABOVE: *The three-story home and surrounding grounds embrace about an acre of Los Cabos' rare swimmable beachfront.* OPPOSITE TOP: *The living room is centered around a floor-to-ceiling fireplace with raised hearth.* INSET: *Numerous sets of sliding glass doors open the interior living/dining area to the huge water-view veranda.* OPPOSITE BOTTOM: *The distinctive exterior staircase and carved double entry doors only begin to hint at the many special features that await at Casa Palmilla.*

he explains, "but nothing held the potential for unparalleled golf that the Koll property possesses." Carving out fairways and greens amid the dramatic desert, mountain and ocean landscape (while leaving the natural arroyos and cactus forests untouched), Nicklaus has created an 18-hole championship course, another nine holes designed around Palmilla's lakes, and an 18-hole putting course within walking distance of the hotel. Golfers are wisely cautioned about Mountain Hole #3, where 400-year-old cacti guard the green; and Hole #5, where your approach to the green must carry over one of the resort's largest arroyos, but stop short of a riverbed just beyond the hole. But this is as demanding as life will ever get here.

The vision that Donald Koll brought to Los Cabos eight years ago is now realized in far more than a world-class resort. Beyond the tropical gardens of his seaside retreat, private places such as Casa Palmilla are ensuring that the landscape and the lifestyle will remain among the most treasured in the world.

Photography by Peter Darley Miller.

Casa Palmilla was presented in Unique Homes by Palmilla Properties, Newport Beach, CA.

CHARACTERISTICS

Property size: One beachfront acre, with 150 feet on the Sea of Cortez.
Architectural style: Spanish Colonial.
Year built: 1986.
Living space: 10,000 square feet.
Number of bedrooms: Five.
Number of baths: Five.
Outbuildings: Boat house, garage with office, separate staff accommodations.
Highlights: Three master suites, view-oriented verandas, recreation room with pool table, five-minute walk to world-renowned Hotel Palmilla.

Villa in Paradise

Lanikai, Kailua, Hawaii

Long before Hawaii placed its proud star on the United States flag, Gary Chikasuye, a native from the islands, took his Harvard degree to New York and began a practice in architecture, working with such firms as Harrison and Abramovitz, Skidmore, Owens and Merrill, and Edward Durrell Stone. In 1972, Gary became director of architecture for yet another renowned firm, Gruen Associates, where he directed a staff of 400 architects. In the course of his 40 years in New York, he was involved in the design of a number of prominent landmarks, including the United Nations, the World Trade Center, Lincoln Center for the Performing Arts and the New York Philharmonic Concert Hall.

In the early 1980s, Gary returned home to Hawaii to reward himself in the island sun and find renewal in what Mark Twain called "the loveliest fleet of islands that lies anchored in any ocean." Whatever notions he might have had about enjoying a well-deserved retirement vanished as fast as the next tide, and soon Gary

OPPOSITE TOP: *A European fountain depicting a mermaid rests in the center of the villa's grand entry courtyard. Colonnaded porticos lining the two wings that emanate from the central core of the residence are reflected in the ground-floor windows, while images of mountains, clouds and palm trees are mirrored in the upper windows.* OPPOSITE BOTTOM: *The second-floor master suite opens to a private deck with views extending over sparkling ocean waters to the Mokulua Islands in the distance.* ABOVE: *Accessible from the living and entertaining areas of the main level is a huge, partially covered lanai. Here, too, the focal point is a 180-degree panorama of islands and ocean.*

Chikasuye was busy designing luxurious homes for many of his friends.

Among his most recent accomplishments is a Mediterranean villa on the southeast coast of Oahu; it is a home at peace amidst a screen of lush vegetation, alone against a horizon of aquamarine, yet just a few miles from the hub of Honolulu. Daylight reflects mountains, passing clouds and towering palms in a facade that is mostly glass. Evening brings on its own native magic as night lights shine on marble, granite, crystal and water. The property itself, over half an acre of prime fee simple land, bespeaks the essence of "aloha" from the mermaid statue

CHARACTERISTICS

Property size: Approximately one-half acre of fee simple land on Lanikai Beach.
Architectural style: Mediterranean villa.
When built: 1990-1992.
Square footage: 6,500.
Number of bedrooms: Four.
Number of baths: Five and one-half.
Outbuildings: Detached guest or staff house with two bedrooms and two baths.
Distinctive features: Colonnaded entrance portico and fountain, extensive European marble and granite, Australian eucalyptus floors, hand-carved floating staircase, ceiling heights of 10 to 20 feet, huge lanai, master suite encompassing entire second story. Unobstructed water and island views throughout.
Additional highlights: Mediterranean-inspired architecture with every modern amenity on Oahu's new "Gold Coast," just north of Honolulu.

enjoying her splash at the entry fountain, to the sweep of warm white sand on Lanikai Beach. The villa is much like a Hawaiian who is "full of aloha"—that is, filled with kindness and compassion, and quick with an embrace for a friend.

Here the architect has created a true looking glass of a home, where grand spaces are divided by settings rather than walls, and windowed planes seem to dissolve into the sea. To the visitor, the perspective is evident at once; upon arriving at the entrance fountain, the eye moves on to the open colonnade, sees straight through to the opposite elevation and the ocean beyond. There are no

OPPOSITE TOP: *After the sun has gone down, night lighting brings a new level of drama to the entrance courtyard.* OPPOSITE BOTTOM: *The gourmet kitchen is as stylish as it is well equipped.* ABOVE: *Set behind a beautifully crafted entry gate, the estate encompasses 22,000 square feet of fee simple land. Immediately to the right upon entering the property is the guest or staff house.*

visual limits, only elements that serve to heighten the dimensions. In the foyer, openness is dramatized by a floating hand-carved staircase and an Austrian chandelier suspended from the 20-foot ceiling. In the master suite, alone on the second floor, elevated views are repeated in surfaces of marble and mirrored glass.

The Mokulua Islands, rising boldly out of the ocean offshore, enhance the spectacular panorama from the formal and informal living rooms, the dining room, media and music centers, and the sun-drenched breakfast room. A huge, partially covered lanai extends the full length of this living space out through sliding glass doors to the ocean breezes. All that surrounds is both magnificent and meditative; here is a setting therapeutic for both mind and soul.

Among Mr. Chikasuye's hallmark touches are the golden floors of Australian eucalyptus, the lustrous marble and granite imported from Italy, Spain and Greece,

crown moldings custom milled for the home, and elaborate marble baths for each of the four bedrooms. On the mechanical side, he has included five zones of air conditioning, a state-of-the-art security system with television monitor entry, an audio system and circulating hot water.

Gary Chikasuye has contributed greatly to some of the most recognized skyscrapers and cultural centers built in America. Yet here, amid the soft rustle of bamboo leaves and the gentle roll of the surf, his design is one of great personal expression. It is a home that speaks well of a master's craft, while honoring its surroundings in the most respectful of ways. It is as full of "aloha" as a native can be.

Photography by Ed Medieros of Central Island Agency Productions.

This villa was presented in Unique Homes by A. Blair Duffy, Jr., Blair Duffy & Associates, Inc., Honolulu, HI.

LEFT: *Window walls surround the formal living room with spectacular views of the ocean.* BELOW: *From the living area, a view to the 20-foot-high entryway, where a "floating" hand-carved staircase leads up to the master suite.* BOTTOM: *In the public areas of the home, rooms are divided by settings rather than walls. Shown here is the dining room which directly overlooks the formal living room.*

Built in the 19th century as part of Britain's ring of land and sea defenses protecting the strategic dockyard at Portsmouth, No Man's Land fort is today the ultimate "island" home, offering unrivaled privacy and security. The seascapes are constantly changing; the rising sun at dawn and the setting sun at dusk produce spectacular backdrops. At night, the lights of the Isle of Wight (less than two miles away) and Portsmouth (about three miles from the fort) constantly shimmer and are only outshone by the brilliant lights of passing ships.

No Man's Land

At the entrance to Portsmouth Harbor

The Solent, England

A monument to Britain's naval supremacy for more than a century, No Man's Land was constructed in the 1860s in an effort to prevent the French from seizing control of the English Channel and landing their troops on the south coast of England. A history of "invasion panic" throughout the 18th century, coupled with an extensive coast vulnerable to attack, prompted the formation of a Royal Commission under Queen Victoria. Its recommendation was to establish two impregnable forts guarding the approaches to Spithead and Portsmouth Harbour. One year after the Fortifications Act of 1860 was passed, work began on the No Man's Land fort—an unprecedented 20-year construction which would cost more than £460,000.

With an overall height of 60 feet and a surface area spanning about three-quarters of an acre, the fort was capable of housing 400 men and some 140,000 pounds of heavy guns. Granite walls and three widths of armour plate (17 inches thick) were to comprise the outer shell; the armour alone is estimated to weigh 6,400 tons. Once completed, there came the subsequent threats of submarines and battleships launched during World War I, and the potential for even greater devastation from long-range bombers in the days of World War II. The fort was continuously strengthened to withstand each frightening new development in wartime technology.

Following the second World War, No Man's Land was deactivated, emptied and left abandoned to stand quietly at sea. It was then that Roger Penfold first caught glimpse of the fort that was to become his home.

A C.P.A. with significant dabblings in residential and commercial building, Penfold had spent his youth sailing and boating these waters. One day he actually went "on board" to have a closer look. "The fort had been terribly vandalized. Brass fittings were ripped apart and smashed. And in places," Penfold described, "the bird mess was over a foot thick! But it certainly presented a chance to break away from the mundane tasks of accounting and construction."

So, in 1986, after Roger Penfold approached the Crown to purchase the long-abandoned fort, No Man's Land began the amazing transformation from forgotten war hero to ultimate island home. The mere size of the structure suggested grand-scale reception and entertaining areas. And its location—accessible only by air or sea—meant extraordinary security and privacy. Where there were once gun stations and secret lookouts, the owner created helicopter pads, a tennis court, indoor swimming pool and sun decks. The Round House, formerly the officers' quarters, is now reserved for the spit-and-polish crew of No Man's Land. The Lighthouse provides the owner's personal accommodations on one main level and two tower floors. And, the fort is supplied with boats, crew uni-

CHARACTERISTICS

Architectural style: Circular English fort of granite and armour-clad construction.

When built: 1861. Converted to a private residence in 1986.

Square footage: Approximately 60,000 (half of which is unconverted).

Number of bedrooms: Five (principal), six (crew).

Number of baths: Six full, two half-baths, plus staff baths.

Distinctive features: Lighthouse offering owner's private quarters, huge circular sun deck, and artifact room with many original fittings. Some furnishings custom designed for the fort. There are two telephone lines, a facsimile interface and an extensive internal phone system.

Additional highlights: This is considered to be one of the largest man-made islands in the world, and it was designed over a hundred years ago to last well into the 21st century.

forms, writing papers and linens, all emblazoned with the crest of No Man's Land.

With the fortitude of a battleship and the finesse of a luxury liner, No Man's Land is as self-sufficient as it is pampering. In addition to the boiler and generator rooms, workshops and a water purification plant, the fort offers provisions for clay pigeon shooting, a gymnasium, billiards room, formal parlours, cozy firesides and custom

OPPOSITE: *The renovation of No Man's Land has resulted in wonderful spaces for grand entertaining. Pictured here, the dining room can comfortably accommodate over 20 for dinner.* LEFT: *Situated above the sunken sun deck is the lighthouse. Its three floors of interior space include the owner's bedroom suite and study as well as two guest suites, a sitting room with fireplace, and a kitchen. Also pictured here are the helicopter pad and the enclosed pool area.*

furnishings. A 30-foot Wellcraft Scarab boat capable of nearly 70 m.p.h. provides swift passage to Portsmouth, three miles away, and an international-class sailboat stands ready for recreational boating.

On one of the largest man-made islands in the world, Roger Penfold has converted a national treasure into a home designed solely for fun and private indulgence. And it is anything but mundane.

No Man's Land was presented in Unique Homes by Brian C. Schmitt, Coldwell Banker Schmitt Real Estate, Marathon, FL, in cooperation with Knight Frank & Rutley, London, England.

The only home that we can't sell
is the home that's not for sale.

Luxury Homes, Inc.
REALTORS®

NORTHERN TRUST PLAZA
301 YAMATO ROAD–SUITE 3150
BOCA RATON, FL 33431

407/997-8388
407/241-9634 FAX

BOCA BANK CORPORATE CENTRE
7000 W. PALMETTO PARK ROAD–SUITE 108
BOCA RATON, FL 33433

407/395-9800
407/395-4385 FAX

800/245-8987

Elite 200

As of August 15th, 1992, the following real estate professionals have been named
to the Unique Homes Elite roster for 1993.
In all, 200 luxury property experts will be honored in the special Elite 200 issue
published by Unique Homes in January 1993.
Those mentioned below and those subsequently added to the roster represent the brokers and agents
who have proven themselves to be leaders in their respective luxury real estate markets.

ARIZONA
Ellie Shapiro, Coldwell Banker-Success Realty, Phoenix

CALIFORNIA
Bonnie Adams, Coldwell Banker, La Jolla
Mary Bookman, The Prudential Lurtsema, Stockton
DeAna Brankovic, Kent Realtors, Marina Del Rey
Faye Carlson, Coldwell Banker, Fremont
Loretta Ferraro, The Prudential California Realty, Sausalito
Else Fuller, Fairbanks Ranch Realty, Rancho Sante Fe
Bernice Gershon, Coldwell Banker, Beverly Hills
Sara Hinman/David Hirschler, Coast Newport Properties, Newport Beach
Phyllis Reed, The Prudential Rodeo Realty, Palos Verdes
Kathy Stevens, Unique Properties, Anderson

COLORADO
Rita Hansen, Metro Brokers, Evergreen
George Harvey, Jr., Nevasca Realty, Telluride

CONNECTICUT
Bill Andruss, Coldwell Banker/Schlott, Greenwich
Evan Baker, Coldwell Banker/Schlott, Fairfield
Joan Carroll, Coldwell Banker/Schlott, Greenwich
Dolores Dean, Coldwell Banker/Schlott, Stamford
Bob Gibbons, Tilghman & Frost, Wilton
Mila Grieb, Mila Grieb Village Realty, Westport
Betty Jensen/Melanie Willard, Jensen-Willard Real Estate, Southport
Evelyn Kahn, Coldwell Banker/Schlott, Greenwich
Jack Marker, Coldwell Banker/Schlott, Greenwich
Suzan Rose, Coldwell Banker/Schlott, Greenwich
June Rosenthal, Juner Properties, Stamford
Sulli Seger, Coldwell Banker/Schlott, New Canaan
Jane Tesei, Coldwell Banker/Schlott, Greenwich
Ann Wilson, Coldwell Banker/Schlott, Ridgefield

FLORIDA
Debra Duvall, Premier Realty Group, Stuart
Pamela E. Hagan, Arvida Realty, Long Boat Key
George E. Lindman, Premier Realty Group, Stuart
Chris McDevitt, RE/MAX Properties, Sarasota
Dale White, The Prudential Florida Realty, Miami

HAWAII
John and Takako Ferry, Bali Hai Realty, Kauai
Karen Jeffery, Pacific Island Investments, Waikoloa

MAINE
Kim Swan-Bennett, The Swan Agency, Bar Harbor

MASSACHUSETTS
Lee Sullivan/Richard Eble, Coldwell Banker-
 Atlantic Realty, Brewster
John Cotton, Jr., Cotton Real Estate, Osterville

NEW JERSEY
Sharon Clayton, Clayton Realtors, Bayhead
Pauline Derrick, Coldwell Banker/Schlott, Mendham
Mary G. Horn, Weichert, Realtors, Morristown
Lynn Brescia, Coldwell Banker/Schlott, Wyckoff
Peggy Mahoney, Coldwell Banker/Schlott, Saddle River
Lindy Peteet, Weichert, Realtors, Mendham
Roy Scott/Robert Oquist, RE/MAX Gold, Short Hills

NEW MEXICO
Paul Johnson, Century 21-Norris Romero Realty, Taos

NEW YORK
Bzee Durfee, Coldwell Banker/Schlott, Bedford Village
Judy Gottesman, Coldwell Banker/Schlott, Huntington
Scott M. and Marilyn M. Stiefvater, The Prudential-Stiefvater, Pelham
Cindy Van Schaack, Towne & Country Properties, Tuxedo Park
Larry Weinstein, RE/MAX Spoonriver Real Estate, New City

NORTH CAROLINA
Owen Gwyn, North Carolina Estates, Research Triangle Park

OREGON
Vicki Bell, Professional 100 Inc., Clackamas

RHODE ISLAND
Claus Rossin, Buffum & Rossin Realty Inc., Westerly

SOUTH CAROLINA
Henry Chambers, Beaufort Realty Company, Beaufort

TEXAS
Sarah Lee Marks, Howell Properties, Houston

VERMONT
Brooks Barron, Brooks Barron Real Estate, Rochester
Barbara West, Quechee Associates, Quechee

VIRGINIA
Jeanne Hockaday, Virginia Country Real Estate, Ordinary
Caroline Rocco, Coldwell Banker, McLean

WASHINGTON
Drina McCorkle, Windermere Real Estate, Anacortes

WASHINGTON, D.C.
Barbara Casey, Coldwell Banker
Donna Evers, Evers & Company Real Estate

CANADA
Anne Richardson, Coldwell Banker-Colt Realty, Victoria, BC

If you're thinking of moving to Dallas, think RE/MAX Northwest, REALTORS®.

We Know Dallas
America's second-
ranked business city,
according to *Fortune*
magazine, Dallas is on a
healthy rebound, and continues to
attract buyers with home prices that are well below
the national average, a strong economic climate,
and a great quality of life.

We Know the Market
Established in 1980 and committed to the highest standards of performance
and integrity, RE/MAX Northwest, REALTORS® is staffed by full-time real
estate professionals (no part-timers) with an average of nine years' experience.

We Know We Can Find the Right Home for You
There are a number of prestigious developments, such as the gate-
guarded community of Stonebriar (pictured here). Complete with
an 18-hole golf course, tennis courts, a 52,000-square-foot
clubhouse with Olympic-size pool, and homes priced from
$200,000 to $2 million, Stonebriar is typical of the
quality addresses we can show you in the
Dallas area.

For more information or a
relocation package, give Todd
Jackson a call and let him
introduce you to all that
awaits in Dallas.

RE/MAX
Northwest, REALTORS®
1933 E. Frankford Road, Suite 100
Carrolton (Dallas), Texas 75007
Office: (214) 492-6262
Fax: (214) 492-4129

DOLPHINS

◆◆◆◆◆◆◆◆◆

*One of the most stirring sights at sea is
dolphins effortlessly gliding through
blue waters.*

*Sculptor Lee Knoll has captured the strength
and beauty of these gifted creatures in this
breathtaking table.*

*Cast in bronze, this limited edition table is
as functional as it is beautiful.*

*Numbers are limited. Various finishes are
available, as are other castable materials.
Custom work is also available.
Call for details.*

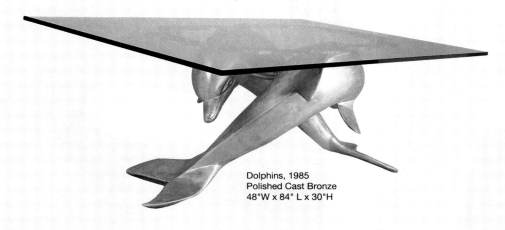

Dolphins, 1985
Polished Cast Bronze
48"W x 84" L x 30"H

LEE KNOLL

*2123 PENN AVENUE
WEST LAWN, PA 19609
215 678-0884*

*The Pleasure of Your Company
is Requested*

*You are cordially invited to join us for a
full year (six issues) of* UNIQUE HOMES *–
your entrée to the finest in available
residential and investment properties.
Your annual subscription will cost
just $24.97–a full 40% off
the newsstand price of $6.95 per issue.*

Call Toll-free 1-800-827-0660